CROSS-CURRICULAR TEACHING AND LEARNING IN THE SECONDARY SCHOOL

THE ARTS

The school curriculum is a contested arena. There are competing pressures from those who advocate that it should be constructed on a subject specific basis, whereas at the other end of the continuum is the stance taken by this book, that learning, and especially learning in the arts, can transcend artificial boundaries between subjects. This book sets out a case for cross-curricular learning involving the arts in secondary schools where teaching and learning really matter.

Cross-Curricular Teaching and Learning in the Secondary School ... The Arts argues for the development of a new, skilful pedagogy which embeds an authentic, cross-curricular approach to teaching and learning in the work of the individual teacher. This approach respects and builds on individual subject cultures within the arts, whilst embracing and exploring links between subject knowledge and subject pedagogies in an enriching way. It focuses on the powerful nature of cross-curricular thinking to produce a joined-up model of teaching and learning where teachers are empowered to think about creative pedagogies, and pupils are able to engage in deep learning as a result.

Key features of the text include:

- Theoretical examination of key issues
- Curriculum planning materials and resources
- A wide range of case studies drawn from innovative practice
- Frameworks for assessment and evaluation.

Part of the *Cross-Curricular Teaching and Learning in the Secondary School* series, this textbook breaks the boundaries between curriculum subjects and the arts. It is timely reading for all students on Initial Teacher Training courses as well as practising teachers looking to introduce cross-curricular themes in their own subjects.

Martin Fautley is Professor of Education at Birmingham City University. He teaches on a range of teacher training and research programmes. His research interests lie in the areas of creativity in education and assessment, and of their role in developing teaching, learning and the curriculum.

Jonathan Savage is Senior Lecturer in Music Education at the Institute of Education, Manchester Metropolitan University. He is also a Visiting Research Fellow at the Royal Northern College of Music, and teaches on a range of PGCE courses and doctoral studies programmes. He is an active researcher in a wide range of areas relating to education and ICT and has research interests in curriculum development.

Cross-Curricular Teaching and Learning in . . .
Series Editor: Jonathan Savage (Manchester Metropolitan University, UK)

The *Cross-Curricular* series, published by Routledge, argues for a cross-curricular approach to teaching and learning in secondary schools. It provides a justification for cross-curricularity across the Key Stages, exploring a range of theoretical and practical issues through case studies drawn from innovative practices across a range of schools. The books demonstrate the powerful nature of change that can result when teachers allow a cross-curricular 'disposition' to inspire their pedagogy. Working from a premise that there is no curriculum development without teacher development, the series argues for a serious re-engagement with cross-curricularity within the work of the individual subject teacher, before moving on to consider collaborative approaches for curriculum design and implementation through external curriculum links.

Cross-curricular approaches to teaching and learning can result in a powerful, new model of subject-based teaching and learning in the high school. This series places the teacher and their pedagogy at the centre of this innovation. The responses that schools, departments or teachers make to government initiatives in this area may be sustainable only over the short term. For longer-term change to occur, models of cross-curricular teaching and learning need to become embedded within the pedagogies of individual teachers and, from there, to inform and perhaps redefine the subject cultures within which they work. These books explore how this type of change can be initiated and sustained by teachers willing to raise their heads above their 'subject' parapet and develop a broader perspective and vision for education in the twenty-first century.

Forthcoming titles in the series:

Cross-Curricular Teaching and Learning in the Secondary School . . . The Arts
Martin Fautley and Jonathan Savage

Cross-Curricular Teaching and Learning in the Secondary School . . . English
David Stevens

Cross-Curricular Teaching and Learning in the Secondary School . . . Foreign Languages
Gee Macrory, Cathy Brady and Sheila Anthony

Cross-Curricular Teaching and Learning in the Secondary School . . . Humanities
Richard Harris and Simon Harrison

Cross-Curricular Teaching and Learning in the Secondary School . . . Using ICT
Maurice Nyangon

Cross-Curricular Teaching and Learning in the Secondary School . . . Mathematics
Robert Ward-Penny

CROSS-CURRICULAR TEACHING AND LEARNING IN THE SECONDARY SCHOOL

THE ARTS

Drama, Visual Art, Music and Design

Martin Fautley and Jonathan Savage

Routledge
Taylor & Francis Group

LONDON AND NEW YORK

This first edition published 2011
by Routledge
2 Park Square, Milton Park, Abingdon, Oxon, OX14 4RN

Simultaneously published in the USA and Canada
by Routledge
270 Madison Avenue, New York, NY 10016

Routledge is an imprint of the Taylor & Francis Group, an informa business

© 2011 Martin Fautley and Jonathan Savage

Typeset in Bembo by
Saxon Graphics Ltd, Derby
Printed and bound in Great Britain by
TJ International Ltd, Padstow, Cornwall

British Library Cataloguing in Publication Data
A catalogue record for this book is available from the British Library

Library of Congress Cataloging-in-Publication Data
Fautley, Martin.
Cross-curricular teaching and learning in the secondary school-- the arts : drama, visual art, music, and design / by Martin Fautley and Jonathan Savage.
p. cm. -- (Cross-curricular teaching and learning in--)
1. Arts--Study and teaching (Secondary)--Great Britain. 2. Education, Secondary--Curricula--Great Britain. 3. Interdisciplinary approach in education--Great Britain. I. Savage, Jonathan. II. Title.
NX280.F38 2011
707.1'241--dc22
2010025702

ISBN13: 978-0-415-55044-4 (hbk)
ISBN13: 978-0-415-55045-1 (pbk)
ISBN13: 978-0-203-83490-9 (ebk)

Contents

List of illustrations

Figures

Tables

Abbreviations

AfL	Assessment for Learning
APP	Assessing Pupils' Progress
ARG	Assessment Reform Group
C Standards	Core standards
CD	Compact disc
CPD	Continuing professional development
DfEE	Department for Education and Employment
DJ	Disc jockey
FMS	Federation of Music Services
GCSE	General Certificate of Secondary Education
H-creative	Historically creative
ICT	Information and communication technologies
IQ	Intelligence quotient
ITT	Initial teacher training
KS	Key Stage
MC	Master of Ceremonies
MIDI	Musical instrument digital interface
n.d.	No date
NACCCE	National Advisory Committee on Creative and Cultural Education
NAME	National Association of Music Educators
NASAGA	North American Simulation and Gaming Association
NCC	National Curriculum Council
NFER	National Foundation for Educational Research
Ofsted	Office for Standards in Education, Children's Services and Skills
PCK	Pedagogic content knowledge
P-creative	Psychologically creative
PGCE	Postgraduate Certificate in Education
PLTS	Personal, learning and thinking skills
Q Standards	Qualified teacher status standards
QCA	Qualifications and Curriculum Authority

QCDA	Qualifications and Curriculum Development Agency
RE	Religious education
SEAL	Social and emotional aspects of learning
S-R	Stimulus-Response
SSAT	Specialist Schools and Academies Trust
TA	Teacher assessment
TDA	Training and Development Agency
TEEVE	Tele-immersive Environment for EVErybody
UK	United Kingdom
WPU	Witness protection unit
ZPD	Zone of proximal development

1

Introduction: the context for cross-curricular teaching and learning

Key objectives

This chapter will introduce a number of key themes for cross-curricular teaching and learning. By the end of this chapter you will have:

- Defined what is meant by a cross-curricular approach to teaching and learning
- Thought about knowledge, and considered what knowledge means in a variety of contexts
- Reflected on the cross-curricular dimensions contained within the National Curriculum
- Considered planning for learning
- Begun to think about the role of assessment
- Considered the key role of creativity
- Reflected on the nature of self and identity

What is cross-curricular teaching and learning?

A cross-curricular approach to teaching is characterised by sensitivity towards, and a synthesis of, knowledge, skills and understandings from various subject areas. These inform an enriched pedagogy that promotes an approach to learning which embraces and explores this wider sensitivity through various methods.

(Savage 2011: 8–9)

This book is about cross-curricular approaches to teaching and learning in the arts. It does not stand alone. As part of a series of books on cross-curricularity in secondary education, it forms an integral part of a web of ideas drawn from the work of eight authors and teachers – each with their own subject allegiances and backgrounds – who have found cross-curricularity to be a vital, driving aspect of their work in recent years.

This definition for a cross-curricular approach to teaching and learning is drawn from the generic title which forms the basis for this series of books (Savage 2011). Key words within this definition, such as *sensitivity*, refer to the ways in which teachers should approach the knowledge, skills and understanding inherent within every curriculum *subject*. Each curriculum *subject* is exemplified in curriculum documents but also has a historical legacy that is underpinned in various ways, not least in teachers' and others' conceptions about a particular *subject* and how it should be taught. Understanding this is a vital step that needs to be taken before moving into collaborative curriculum ventures. Cross-curricular approaches are about *synthesising* ideas, but this should not be done in a way that destroys the cherished ideas and ways of thinking that every *subject* contains. Rather, this definition for cross-curricularity encourages the development of an *enriched* pedagogy that a skilful teacher can adopt for the explicit purposes of enhancing teaching and learning. The new, *enriched* pedagogy of cross-curricular teaching will *embrace* and *explore* the teacher's *sensitivity* towards, and *synthesis* of, the different knowledge, skills and understanding within curriculum *subjects*. In order for this to happen, there are at least two premises: first, teachers will need to understand their own intrinsic, and their subject's, 'subjectivities'; second, teachers will need to ensure that their subject knowledge is extended beyond their own subject areas. When this occurs, teachers will be in a position to develop a cross-curricular approach to learning that utilises a range of methods or techniques in line with the following principles and purposes.

What cross-curricular teaching and learning in the arts entails

A key question for educators is how to organise schools so that learning and teaching are most effective. New ways of teaching and learning, and new ways of knowing, are part of the constant technological revolution that is the constant backdrop against which twenty-first century young people will conduct their lives. This revolution in information, where the Internet means that a huge amount of information and content is available at the touch of a few keys has changed the way society thinks about knowledge, and, importantly, what it means to 'know'. In this book we shall consider how cross-curricularity in the arts can be at the forefront of developments, and how such matters as personalisation, collaboration, and creativity can be nurtured in young people in schools, colleges and society generally. To do this we shall consider what learning and knowledge are, how they can best be fostered and developed, what the roles of the teacher are in this, and how best to develop the individual students towards their maximum potential. This sometimes involves asking some difficult questions, and we shall not shy away from doing this!

Let us begin by considering what cross-curricular teaching and learning in, and through, the arts entails. To do this we need to start by exploring the notion of curriculum, in order to understand how the current situation arose, and what it might mean to contemporary understandings of the way we organise learning and teaching. According to Bernstein,

Formal educational knowledge can be considered through three message systems: curriculum, pedagogy and evaluation. Curriculum defines what counts as valid knowledge, pedagogy defines what counts as a valid transmission of knowledge, and evaluation defines what counts as a valid realization of this knowledge …

(Bernstein 1971: 47)

This notion of 'what counts as valid knowledge' is an important one for us here. We shall, in the course of this book, consider the various aspects raised by Bernstein, of knowledge, of pedagogy, and of evaluation, which for our purposes in today's climate we shall consider alongside assessment. However, to return to our discussion of curriculum, the ways in which it is organised vary from country to country, from region to region, and from school to school. We also that know that:

> ... curriculum is inextricably linked to social context. Broad historical, cultural, economic and political forces inter-relate to form and shape teaching and learning.
>
> (Moon and Murphy 1999: 1)

What this means for us is that the way things are organised will be different according to time and place. Let us begin by considering some particular aspects which relate to you, the reader, with regard to this.

Reflective task

Part 1: What is your job title? Are you, for example, a 'teacher of art', or maybe 'head of drama'? Is this all you do?

Part 2: What route did you take to get to this position? What qualifications did you take at school? What subject is your degree in?

How do these relate? Have you followed a linear pathway and career route, or have there been other things you have done along the way?

Historical note

In the UK, the National Curriculum was for many years seen as the defining feature of school curricular organisation, or according to some, a straitjacket for the containment and demarcation of knowledge. The original architects of the National Curriculum decided which subjects would be included – ten in total – and then gave the job of deciding what would be included in each of the ten subjects to ten different authoring committees.

> ... the National Curriculum was set up subject by subject through a series of working parties. Cross referencing between working parties, made up of government nominees, was discouraged and the setting up and reporting took place at different times ...
>
> (Moon 1995: 257)

The arts were viewed as separate subjects by the original designers, with art and music, but not drama or dance, included in it. However, the very inclusion of art and music was contested at the time. Tony Taylor writes of how the then education secretary, Kenneth Baker, was 'furious' at the then prime minister's (Margaret Thatcher) attempt to '... drop art and music from the curriculum' (Taylor 1999: 42). Art and music remained, but, owing to the complexities outlined by Bob Moon above, had virtually nothing to do with each other. Indeed, in the case of music, the content of the programme of study for the National Curriculum was subject to some vitriolic exchanges, played out mostly in the pages of the national press:

> Despite the opposition of many leading music educators and musicians, led by conductor Simon Rattle, the curriculum was weighted towards musical theory and appreciation rather than practical activities.
>
> (Moon 1995: 258)

We shall revisit the introduction of the National Curriculum in Chapter 2, but for the moment we need to note this concern for the content of curriculum reminds us that education is a political issue, and that content of curriculum, Bernstein's 'valid knowledge', has to be decided by someone. This begs the question: whose knowledge is valid? What makes it so, and who are the validators? Owing to the fragmented way in which the National Curriculum was drawn up, opportunities for cross-curricular linkages, or even for commonalities between subjects, were distinctly limited. However, there were *cross-curricular themes*, and these were designed to be spread across all subjects, and consisted of

> ... elements that enrich the educational experience of pupils. They are more structured and pervasive than any other cross-curricular provision and include a strong component of knowledge and understanding in addition to skills. Most can be taught through other subjects as well as through themes and topics.
>
> (NCC 1989: 6)

The cross-curricular themes they were referring to included economic and industrial understanding, health education, environmental education and citizenship. In addition to cross-curricular themes, there were also *cross-curricular skills*, which included communication, numeracy, problem solving, information technology and study skills. A problem at the time was that these were seen as something of a 'bolt on' accessory, rather than central to the curriculum. There was a concern that this would lead to these elements not receiving the attention they deserved:

> The sheer rate of change that is taking place in education is unprecedented. The volume of paper reaching schools and requiring responses is daunting, even to the most committed professional. The core and other foundation subjects are currently centre-stage. Unless teachers and schools are vigilant, the benefits of cross-curricular themes could be adversely affected.
>
> (Pumfrey 1993: 21)

The atomistically designed National Curriculum meant that there just was not enough time to deal with the cross-curricular themes and skills. As David Hargreaves observed:

> ... greater breadth was a key purpose behind the National Curriculum reforms. As all teachers know, the broader the curriculum becomes, the greater the problem of manageability. The problem is easily stated: how to get the quart of a desirable

curriculum into the pint pot of the school timetable … How, then, did they [the curriculum designers] achieve the trick of getting the quart into the pint pot? By sleight of hand, of course …

(Hargreaves 1991: 36)

The 'sleight of hand' to which Hargreaves refers was by telling teachers that they could teach all of the themes through existing subjects, even though teachers were complaining that there was too much content already, and the committees who had designed the content had not included the extra material. The result of this led to what Bob Moon called 'complex and retrospective attempts to achieve cross-curricular coherence' (Moon 1995: 259). It is likely that these early problems clouded the ways in which teachers thought about cross-curricular matters, and this has, to some extent, caused some teachers to retreat into entrenched subject-based positions in order to make sense of their workloads.

However, recent curricular developments have freed this up to a considerable extent, with the latest version of the National Curriculum being explicit about being amenable to local variations. What this has meant is that the old ways can now be challenged and rethought, which is precisely what we will be doing in this book.

Curriculum development and the teacher

Reflective task

In the last reflective task, we asked you to think about your current position, and the route you took to arrive at it.

Now, think about how much of your current position entails dealing with things *other* than your main subject. Do you, for example, teach aspects of literacy? Of numeracy? Maybe you have to deal with personal and social aspects of learning, for example in dealing with group work? What else do you do?

It is likely that you do a wide range of things beyond your subject specialism!

In the accompanying over-arching book to this one (Savage 2011), three key themes are suggested which have a significant impact upon curriculum. Summarised briefly, these are:

1. What is meant by 'curriculum development' and could it be linked to my own development as a teacher?

2. Why is it important to develop a sense of my own 'subjectivity' and how would this relate to curriculum development and the construction of a skilful pedagogy underpinned by reflective practice?

3. How explicitly are learning and teaching linked together?

From these three themes, a number of significant issues emerge which we shall consider with relation to cross-curricular work in the arts.

This section began by asking you to think about the multiplicity of aspects to your current role which can be seen to be beyond the subject specific. This was purposefully undertaken in order to establish the breadth of roles which teaching entails. Indeed, we can go further:

Reflective task

One PGCE course leader says teaching involves the following roles:

Nanny; Lawyer; Referee; Mediator; Supporter; Role Model; Advisor; Guide; Police Officer; Probation Officer; Judge; Counsellor; Social Worker; Mentor; Moderator; Coach; Director; Jailer; Facilitator; Leader; Supporter; Confessor; Pacifier; Trail Blazer; Motivator; Controller.[1]

How many of these roles have you fulfilled recently?

In order to undertake these you will have received some training, either in initial teaching training (ITT), as a result of continuing professional development (CPD), or, quite possibly, no training at all, and these are things which you have had to pick up as best as you can en route. This takes us to the first of the three general principles above, possibly expounded best by Laurence Stenhouse, who observed that there can be 'no curriculum development without teacher development' (Stenhouse 1980: 85). Stenhouse placed the teacher firmly at the centre of educational development and reform, and it is this principle which clearly derives from the first of the three key themes above. We began this chapter by thinking about curriculum, and curriculum development is a key theme of this book. Curriculum development, as Stenhouse observed, begins with the teacher, and so we have been thinking, and will continue to think about your role in this, and what you could do to develop yourself in terms of your teaching, and the curriculum. This thought takes us to the second of our main principles, that of pedagogy.

Pedagogy

The notion of pedagogy is an important one, and will form one of the central components of this book. The classification of pedagogy we will be using is this:

Pedagogy is the art and science of teaching.

Whether you are a beginning or an established teacher, you will have be developing your own pedagogy, and will have evolved a variety ways of ways in which you teach various topics. We will discuss pedagogy in detail in Chapter 3, but for the moment it is useful to note that what we are referring to by the terminology includes not only ways in which teaching takes place, but also ways in which your own ideas, knowledge and background impinge upon your teaching. There is an old proverb which states that some people have five years of experience, others have one year's experience five times! This can be particularly true in secondary school teaching, with its annual cycle of timetables delineating regular teaching and learning. We want you to build upon your experiences, and add to them, and so although pedagogy will feature consistently in our discussions, we hope that this will also be enacted in your professional practice, that you will be trying out new ideas, and reflecting upon what you have done.

Learning and teaching

A common lament in staffrooms is 'I don't know why they haven't learned it, I've taught it to them a thousand times!' This cry neatly sums up the issue. Teaching does not entail a direct one-to-one mapping onto learning. If it did, people would only need teaching something once, and it would be there for life. This is clearly not the case, and it can be a mistake to assume that there is a straightforward linear relationship between the two. We shall revisit teaching and learning a number of times in later chapters, especially Chapter 3, and try to uncover some of the more complex issues that arise, including both theoretical and practical considerations. We shall also be challenging you in a metacognitive fashion to think about your own thinking concerning teaching and learning, how this has been formed and shaped, and how you enact teaching for learning on a daily basis within your professional work.

The National Curriculum in the UK

In the UK, the National Curriculum, as we saw above, is the key framework for organising teaching and learning in schools. We discussed some of the problems that arose with the original version of the National Curriculum, and now we are going to turn our attention to more recent versions, and how they have altered the ways that teaching and learning can be thought about.

Practical task

Without looking at it, can you say what parts of the National Curriculum for your subject are most important a) for you, b) for the students?

The National Curriculum, however, is more than just the specification for the subjects which you teach. Having learned from the problems with the original National Curriculum, the more recent version has provided a common framework for all subjects. This means that when you look at the layout for each subject they are all broadly similar, involving Key Concepts, Key Processes, Range of Study, and Curriculum Opportunities. This allows for ready comparison between subjects, and indeed, the web-based versions encourage the reader to do just that. In addition to this subject-based approach to teaching and learning, the QCDA have developed a 'big picture' of the curriculum (QCDA 2010), which shows that there are a considerable number of curriculum elements which need to be considered, of which individual subjects are but a single component. Each subject has a section entitled 'Wider Opportunities', and this section makes links between the subject in question, and other areas of the curriculum. These elements are part of the subject orders, and so in that sense can be considered as statutory.

Aside from subjects, other elements which go to make up 'the big picture' are non-statutory 'cross-curricular dimensions'. These include:

- Identity and cultural diversity
- Healthy lifestyles
- Community participation
- Enterprise
- Global dimensions and sustainable development
- Technology and the media
- Creativity and critical thinking

As was the case with earlier iterations of the National Curriculum, some teachers tend to have a sceptical view of these, viewing them as 'bolt-on' accessories to the main business of subject teaching. But let us take time to consider the implications of cross-curricular dimensions on subject teaching. The QCDA (then QCA) said this of the dimensions:

> The cross-curriculum dimensions reflect some of the major ideas and challenges that face individuals and society, and help make learning real and relevant.
> The dimensions are unifying areas of learning that span the curriculum and help young people make sense of the world. They are not curriculum subjects, but are crucial aspects of learning that should permeate the curriculum and the life of a school.
>
> (QCA 2009: 1)

This raises all sorts of issues! The dimensions contain major ideas, but are non-statutory, they help 'young people make sense of the world', but they lie outside subjects. But once we get past the scepticism we can see that these are things which we would want our learners to be. Let us try to unpick some of the details, as a precursor to our more detailed thinking in later chapters.

As an example, let us take the issue of identity and cultural diversity. This dimension, the QCDA says, will help young people:

- develop their own sense of belonging and self-esteem
- recognise the value of diversity within and between identities, groups and communities
- understand the multiple and shared identities, beliefs, cultures, traditions and histories of the people in the UK, and recognise that these have shaped and continue to shape life here
- understand the importance of human rights and the consequences of intolerance and discrimination, and know how to challenge these
- understand the need for everyone living in a democracy to participate in decision-making

- understand the factors that influence and change places, communities and wider society, such as migrations, economic inequality and conflicts
- recognise the UK's changing relationship and interconnections with the rest of the world
- critically reflect on the shared and diverse values in society

(QCA 2009: 11)

Some of these seem like big topics, and far broader than a single curriculum area can deal with. Yet the arts are in many ways the ideal place for some of these big questions to find a home. Let us take the first bullet as a case in point. Issues of self-esteem are important in our young people.

The self, and identity

Feeling a sense of self-worth and confidence can be fostered and engendered through collaborative work in the arts, almost unlike any other subject area. Here is a teacher talking about cross curricular project work with Year 7 pupils:

> … we don't really have any sort of set testing or anything like that so, in terms of facts and figures it might be difficult to assess pupils' attainment, but certainly we've noticed in lessons that the pupils are gaining in confidence, and the pupils are used to working together in groups. Working in pairs, in small groups, and as a large group, as a whole class. And we find that their confidence is improving and they're quite willing to speak out and share their opinions whereas before, with, you know with previous experience of year sevens they seem to be, you know they seem to be quite shy and perhaps unwilling to voice an opinion in case, you know in case they feel silly about it or if anyone makes a comment about it
>
> (KS3 teacher)

These are powerful sentiments, but then these can be life-changing experiences for the young people!

There are a number of ways in which the issue of self-esteem can be considered in educational terms. One of the most well-known early pieces of work in this domain is that of Maslow, who proposed a hierarchy of needs (Maslow 1954), ranging from basic physiological needs, for example food, drink and air, through to self-actualisation, and reaching one's full potential. In the middle of this hierarchy Maslow placed the need for self-esteem. In fact Maslow divided this into two, *competence*, which he saw as being the need to be confident in front of peers, and the second being *recognition,* which he viewed as the desire to be respected by others. If these needs are not met then feelings of anxiety and inadequacy can result. For students in schools this can manifest itself in the ways pupils think about themselves, and express thoughts about themselves, or, in some cases, fear of expressing themselves for fear of ridicule.

> Low self-esteem means a negative sense of self. It may be openly expressed ('I'm useless', 'I don't matter', 'I'm a failure'), or it may be an underlying sense of inadequacy or worthlessness that is hard to put into words. Low self-esteem is neither an …

emotional disorder nor a personality disorder ... but rather an element of many different presenting problems.

(Fennell and Jenkins 2004: 413)

For many teachers, working to enhance student self-esteem is an important aspect of the work they do. For students with low self-esteem, tasks which allow them to succeed are often seen to be important in engaging them with the learning process. Some students with low self-esteem would in some cases prefer to give up on tasks early on, rather than fear failing at them. For this reason constructing learning encounters which allow children to 'fail safely' is often a key component in the design of cross-curricular learning encounters.

Related to the notion of self-esteem is that of self-efficacy. Self-efficacy was described by Bandura as

... people's judgements of their capabilities to organize and execute courses of action required to attain designated types of performances. It is concerned not with the skills one has but with the judgements of what one can do with whatever skills one possesses.

(Bandura 1986: 391)

This makes an important distinction from self-esteem, as here the concern is with how the individual feels about their ability to perform in various areas. This affects motivation too: 'Efficacy beliefs influence how people feel, think. motivate themselves, and behave' (Bandura 1993: 118). From the perspective of thinking about cross-curricular learning, it is appropriate to consider learning activities which help students develop their feelings of self-efficacy as potentially helpful. This is not only intrinsically worthwhile, but as Zimmerman notes:

... self-efficacious students participate more readily, work harder, persist longer, and have fewer adverse emotional reactions when they encounter difficulties than do those who doubt their capabilities.

(Zimmerman 2000: 86)

Considering the self-efficacy of students is an appropriate backdrop to a consideration of cross-curricular learning encounters which develop supportive and cooperative ways for pupils to learn together.

Teacher identity

In addition to considering the fostering of self-esteem and self-efficacy in students, it will also be the case that some of the material in this book might challenge the conceptions you hold of your own identity as a teacher. The first reflective task in this chapter asked you, in essence, to label yourself. This produced a labelled identity of yourself as 'Head of Maths', or whatever. But some of you will have said 'teacher of children', or something similar. This is a different identity, and shows you think of yourself in this light. So, what is a teacher identity?

> Teacher professional identity then stands at the core of the teaching profession. It provides a framework for teachers to construct their own ideas of 'how to be', 'how to act' and 'how to understand' their work and their place in society. Importantly, teacher identity is not something that is fixed nor is it imposed; rather it is negotiated through experience and the sense that is made of that experience.
>
> (Sachs 2005: 15)

The point to note here is Sachs's observation that 'teacher identity is not something that is fixed nor is it imposed', this means the identity you hold as a teacher is subject to change. You will have different insights, different views on education, and different feelings about how things work over time, both as a result of the accumulation of experience, and of changing views. The way in which you function as a teacher, and the identities you have constructed for yourself might be challenged, possibly threatened, or affirmed by some of the ideas which you come across over time. This point too needs to be borne in mind as we work our way through the some of the ideas and discussions in this book. We shall revisit the notion of teacher identities in Chapter 3.

Organising learning

So far we have been considering the sorts of themes that can be incorporated into cross-curricular teaching and learning. What it is useful to do at this point is to ask four key questions:

- What is it we want pupils to learn?
- How do we want them to learn it?
- What is the best way of making this happen?
- How will you know?

> ### Reflective task
>
> Have you ever stopped and asked yourself these questions?
>
> Do it now. Try to think big, beyond your subject too!

So, what is it we want students to know, and therefore what do we want them to learn? This is a really hard question to answer properly. A simple response is to think about what is required by the National Curriculum, and say 'in my subject they need to know about X, Y and Z'. Is that sufficient? Is what we want pupils to learn solely the topics of the National Curriculum? So we only want them to know about Shakespeare, quadratic equations, volcanoes, Nazis, dissection, mixing colours, and a few other bits too? This seems a very reductive way of dealing with the complex and multifarious issues of world culture. Another approach to this question is to follow a line of reasoning that rethinks 'what is it we want pupils to learn?' and asks 'what sort of people do we want our school leavers to be?'; or, maybe 'what does it mean to be an educated person in the twenty-first century?'. These are all much harder questions! It is entirely likely that the sorts of lists that will result from deliberations in answer to these questions are likely to look very much like the sub-components of the QCDA's cross-curricular dimensions. We want caring, confident, secure individuals, mindful of, and compassionate to, the needs of others, aware of global issues, able to take responsibility, be upstanding citizens, and so on. Knowing about volcanoes (etc.) might help, but there are other issues which are important too, including the strands in individual National Curriculum subjects that refer to cross-curricular teaching and learning.

How do we want them to learn it?

A Victorian era public school headmaster would probably not have felt out of place looking at many secondary school timetables in the closing years of the twentieth century. Learning appeared to be organised into discrete blocks, and allocated time according to its perceived importance. This fairly static model has been broken down in the early years of the twenty-first century in many schools. For example, some schools suspend the timetable on certain days, others have thematic weeks, some merge blocks of subjects into groups, one school has 'funky Fridays' where cross-curricular projects are undertaken, and a few suspend the timetable altogether for new Year 7s, and organise them in a more primary school way to facilitate transfer. The new National Curriculum encourages this, and more and more schools are trying these new ways.

One of the driving forces behind these changes is the notion that learning and knowledge are not itemised, and then categorised into boxes with fixed boundaries. There are topics that cross over a range of subjects. As an example of this thinking, let us take a relatively straightforward construct, that of measuring. There are numerous ways in which measuring occurs in subjects:

- measuring the width of the margin to draw in an exercise book
- measuring distances on maps
- measuring how far a javelin has been thrown
- calculating how near the Sun is
- weighing of ingredients in food technology
- weighing out tiny quantities of chemicals
- measuring the time it takes to run 100 metres in PE
- thinking about geological time
- counting beats in music
- …and many, many other examples

Measuring is clearly a cross-curricular skill. But who should teach it? Do all the teachers of the subjects involved in the list assume someone else has? Or do they all assume no one has, and teach it again from scratch? Either of these two responses seems wrong, pupils will either be left to work it out for themselves, or waste time repeating things they already know and can do. Certainly there will be subject specific aspects of measuring, ranging from getting out of the way of moving javelins, to using the right tools for weighing tiny amounts of chemicals, but even so, the principle remains. What this discussion is moving towards is the notion of a *curriculum map*. We saw at the beginning of this chapter that the original National Curriculum was drawn up by the separate subject groups in isolation from each other. In many ways that isolationism has remained, and the current National Curriculum, although much more fluid in its subject boundaries, has retained something of the exclusivity of subject delineation of the previous ones. But what is curriculum mapping?

Mapping the curriculum

Working out what bits of knowledge are taught and learned where, when, and by whom, are not as yet common in UK schools. At its simplest, making a map of the curriculum involves heads of departments listing topics taught in units of work, and then taking an overview as to how these fit with other departments, and other units of work across the school. Undertaking this exercise is time-consuming, probably best done using ICT, and requires dedicated time and resources. But, having been done, what is shown can be quite revealing! As Janet Hale notes, 'curriculum mapping is a multifaceted, ongoing process designed to improve student learning' (Hale 2007: 4). If schools find that some topics are being taught on a number of occasions, and others not at all, then this in itself is a useful outcome.

This kind of curriculum planning is encouraged by the National Curriculum. A closer look at individual subject's programmes of study reveal important new emphases on collaborative, cross-subject working. In every subject's 'Wider Opportunities' statements you will find references like:

- Work on problems that arise in other subjects and in contexts beyond the school (Mathematics 4d);
- Develop speaking and listening skills through work that makes cross-curricular links with other subjects (English 4f);
- Make links between science and other subjects and areas of the curriculum (Science 4k); and
- Make links between geography and other subjects, including citizenship and ICT, and areas of the curriculum including sustainability and global dimension (Geography 4i).

These subject references to cross-curricular opportunities are particularly helpful and represent a significant shift in the curriculum orders. They are, of course, statutory and a plethora of advice about how to implement these (and other) changes has been produced for teachers (QCDA 2009).

Alongside the cross-curricular dimensions and the individual subjects' Programmes of Study, there are other statutory elements of the curriculum at Key Stage 3 that all teachers have to embed within their teaching. These include Functional Skills in English, mathematics and ICT, and the Personal, Learning and Thinking Skills (PLTS). Both these sets of skills and competencies will require teachers to make imaginative links between their subject's knowledge, skills and understanding and other areas of knowledge. This has many similarities to what we might consider a more traditional cross-curricular set of teaching and learning approaches.

So, every teacher in every subject at Key Stage 3 is charged with developing a cross-curricular approach to teaching and learning. It is the law.

Case Study: Curriculum Mapping: Topic – Slavery

In one school a chance conversation between the music and history teachers in the staffroom led to them undertaking a single-topic curriculum mapping exercise with regards to the topic of slavery. The music teacher was doing a unit on the origins of the blues with Year 9 pupils, and included a section on the origins of the blues in the work songs of slaves. The history teacher had taught the topic of slavery as a component of Year 8 work. Inquiring across the staff on a wider basis they found that the topic was also taught, or at least touched upon, by a range of subjects, including:

RE: where the moral implications and political implications were discussed, alongside a study of the Moses and the Hebrew slaves in the Old Testament.

Citizenship: Where the effects of post-colonial immigration and pupil identities were discussed.

Geography: Where studies of human geography included a section on the transplantation and forced migration of peoples.

English: where pupils were working on empathetic stories and poems of what it was like to be a slave.

Art: where aspects of slavery as a source of inspiration were investigated.

From a chance conversation a whole area of study was shown to pervade the curriculum!

The example of the slavery topic shown above is but one readily apparent thematic area which figures across a range of subjects. This information would not have been apparent without the teachers concerned seeking it out.

According to Andrew Porter, writing from an American context, there are four ways of looking at the curriculum:

Curriculum can be divided into the intended, enacted, assessed, and learned curricula. For K-12 education, the intended curriculum is captured most explicitly in state content standards— statements of what every student must know and be able to do by some specified point in time. The enacted curriculum refers to instruction (e.g. what happens in classrooms). The assessed curriculum refers to student achievement tests.

(Porter 2006: 141)

These four categorisations are helpful in thinking about the way learning is organised, and the ways in which it actually takes place. The learned curriculum is everything that pupils learn in schools, including everything from when not to run in corridors, to how to go in to assembly. This links to the notion of *the hidden curriculum*, so called because it is not overt, but contains all the incidental things pupils learn at school. There are many other ways of thinking about curriculum. Lave and Wenger (1991) discuss the differences between a *teaching curriculum*, and a *learning curriculum*. In the former, teaching is the main focus of activity, whereas in the latter the main focus is on learning. Hale (2007) distinguishes between the *planned* and the *operational* curriculum. The planned curriculum involves the documentary preparation, units of work, and lesson planning materials produced by teachers, the operational curriculum is what actually comes out from this planning, in the sense that not everything that is planned for pupils to learn actually takes place. This seems to be an issue for schools, especially when the only people who have a knowledge of the full extent of the curriculum map are the pupils, rather than the teachers and school leadership teams!

It should be clear from these discussions that one of the major issues facing cross-curricular thinking is in working out what the existing planned curriculum is in the first place!

Breaking Barriers: The role of the 14-19 Diplomas

It will be no easy feat to establish a curriculum map, but one way which some schools have addressed this issue is to approach the task from a different angle, and plan afresh for extended learning experiences. An example of this is to be found in the UK in the diploma qualification for 14-19 year old students. At the time of writing there are 14 diplomas available, covering the following areas:

- Business, Administration and Finance
- Construction and the Built Environment
- Creative and Media
- Engineering
- Environmental and Land-Based Studies
- Hair and Beauty Studies
- Hospitality
- Information Technology
- Manufacturing and Product Design
- Public Services
- Retail Business
- Society, Health and Development
- Sport and Active Leisure
- Travel and Tourism

As an example of these, let us take the Creative and Media diploma, and think about it from a cross-curricular perspective. To do this, we shall focus on the foundation level qualification. Teaching for the diploma is organised thematically, rather than in a subject-content driven fashion. Indeed, there is an exhortation to teachers to think outside of and beyond traditional subject boundaries

> Teaching of the key themes should reflect the aim of the creative and media Diploma by integrating key themes across the disciplines, rather than taking a 'single-subject' approach.
>
> (QCA n.d.: 7)

The themes concerned are:

- Creativity in context
- Thinking and working creatively
- Principles, processes and practice
- Creative businesses and enterprise

Work on these will encompass studying aspects of :

- art and design: 2D and 3D art, craft, graphic design, product design, fashion and textiles, photo imaging
- performing arts: dance, drama and music
- media: film and television, radio and audio, interactive media, animation, computer games, creative writing, advertising

> (QCA n.d.: 14)

There is an expectation that much of this work is practically based, allowing schools to tailor the provision to suit their own particular needs and requirements, meaning that the specific details of diploma provision will be available to individual schools to develop, working alongside industry partners.

What this brief discussion concerning the diploma has shown is an alternative approach to curriculum mapping. Here the content is decidedly multi-subject and cross-curricular, and so planning takes place from a different starting point, in this case the thematic approaches outlined in the diploma regulations.

Personalising cross-curricular learning

Personalising learning is about making learning relevant for the pupils in schools across the country. It is about personalising that which is learnt for the specific local requirements and needs, and for the abilities and interests of each class. It does not necessarily mean having thirty pupils working on different things at the same time! Here is one influential definition of personalised learning:

Learner-centred and knowledge-centred
Close attention is paid to learners' knowledge, skills, understanding and attitudes. Learning is connected to what they already know (including from outside the

classroom). Teaching enthuses pupils and engages their interest in learning: it identifies, explores and corrects misconceptions. Learners are active and curious: they create their own hypotheses, ask their own questions, coach one another, set goals for themselves, monitor their progress and experiment with ideas for taking risks, knowing that mistakes and 'being stuck' are part of learning. Work is sufficiently varied and challenging to maintain their engagement but not so difficult as to discourage them. This engagement allows learners of all abilities to succeed, and it avoids the disaffection and attention-seeking that give rise to problems with behaviour.

(Gilbert and Teaching and Learning in 2020 Review Group 2006: 6)

The 2020 report also observes that '... Pupils are more likely to be engaged with the curriculum they are offered if they believe it is relevant' (Gilbert and Teaching and Learning in 2020 Review Group 2006: 20). Personalising learning can also be considered as *relevantising*, making learning relevant to the pupils. This means that different approaches and topic areas may be appropriate for learners in the inner cities, whilst different ones may be appropriate for those in the suburbs, and different ones again for those in rural areas. So, what does this mean for cross-curricular learning?

Reflective task

What are the specific locational characteristics of the pupils at your school? Is it urban, rural, affluent, mixed, or what?

How have you adapted what you teach to be suitable for your pupils?

If you can consider a school to be the opposite of some of the characteristics you have described above, how different might you have to make the curriculum?

This is personalising the curriculum, how is it encouraged at your school?

Historically, teachers have often worked out how to teach a specific and predetermined number of units of work, and stick with them. We occasionally hear stories of teachers still teaching units with the old school name on the folder from where they used to teach some years into a new post! This is personalising *teaching*, in the sense that it 'belongs' to that teacher. It is not personalising *learning*, by matching what is being done to the needs of the pupils in that particular school.

Vignette

In Birmingham there is a street with two secondary schools directly facing each other on opposite sides of the road. They are very different schools. Each has its own strengths and priorities. Although so close, units of work are very different in the two schools, and teaching and learning are very different too. Personalising learning means that differences are obvious to anyone visiting.

Assessment

One of the key themes which we shall return to on a number of occasions is that of assessment. In Chapter 6 we discuss this in some detail, but here it is appropriate to note that assessment needs to be considered alongside curriculum design and innovation. This is particularly the case with summative assessment, particularly high-stakes summative assessments which have been externally designated, as the teaching and learning will need to be validated by these. Thus in the case of diplomas the requirements of the awarding bodies will be of primary concern. A less clear-cut relationship occurs at KS3, where National Curriculum assessment is to be carried out in single subject modalities.

Personalising, planning, and assessment

When preparing for personalising learning, and thinking about how best to organise the planned curriculum, the examples we have been discussing provide us with two common models of how this is normally undertaken. In the first model, the curriculum is planned, and the summative assessments which will take place are organised to follow the intended learning. Formative assessment, which, as we shall discuss later, is likely to make a real difference to learning, will be happening throughout the learning process. In the second model, curriculum organisation begins with a consideration of the final summative assessment, and the planned curriculum is then organised so as to deliver learning based on the requirements of the assessment. A diagrammatic representation of this is given in Figure 1.1, which shows the process from the perspective of planning, not delivery.

Neither of these ways is automatically better, but teachers need to be clear in their own minds which of the two models is in operation when they are planning for teaching and learning to take place. We know that assessment is a matter of concern for many teachers, and so being clear about how the work being undertaken is to be organised should help bring a degree of clarity to an already complex situation.

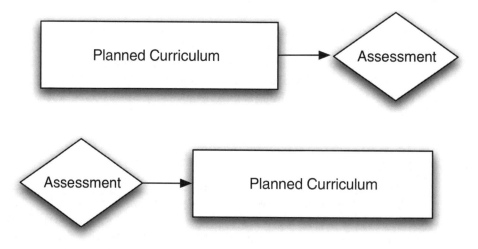

Figure 1.1 Planning and assessment.

Creativity

All of these discussions concerning curriculum mapping, assessment and planning may seem a long way from the excitement that good cross-curricular learning entails, and so let us return to one of the core topics of cross-curricularity in the arts, that of creativity. Creativity and critical thinking figure as one of the cross-curricular dimensions of the National Curriculum. We shall consider creativity and critical thinking separately, beginning with the former.

Reflective task

What is creativity? Do you have a definition you can use? How does it apply in your teaching?

Defining creativity is notoriously complex, and we consider this in some detail in Chapter 2, so to short-circuit this for our present considerations, we shall use the definition of creative processes provided in the National Advisory Committee on Creative and Cultural Education report *All Our Futures*:

> First, they always involve thinking or behaving imaginatively. Second, overall this imaginative activity is purposeful: that is, it is directed to achieving an objective. Third, these processes must generate something original. Fourth, the outcome must be of value in relation to the objective.
>
> (NACCCE 1999: 30)

Creativity, therefore, involves these four processes. What do they mean? Let us consider them each in turn.

Imaginative activity

Imaginative activity occurs when students engage in processes which are generative in nature, they are creating new ideas, seeing things from a different angle, or forming previously unknown connections. This is from the perspective of the individual making the new connections, generating new ideas, or thinking of new associations. It is important here to note that this does not mean that the ideas in question have never been thought of before by anyone, but rather that the new ideas in question are new for that individual. Margaret Boden draws the distinction between creative acts which are new and original for the student in question, and those which are entirely new for anyone. The former she calls *psychologically creative*, abbreviated to P-creative; these are creative ideas which have occurred to an individual, but which the teacher or others may well have encountered before. The latter she calls *historically creative*, or H-creative; these are ideas which are both novel for the individual, and novel in the historical sense that no-one has had them before.

> If Mary Smith has an idea which she could not have had before, her idea is P-creative – no matter how many people have had the same idea already. The historical sense applies to ideas that are fundamentally novel with respect to the whole of human

history. Mary Smith's surprising idea is H-creative if no one has ever had the idea before her.

(Boden 1990: 32)

These are important distinctions for us, as we are able to use them to account for work which the students undertake and produce which is new and novel for them, but which may not be original when viewed from a wider perspective. This allows us to celebrate acts and process of P-creativity as being worthwhile within the contexts in which they are created. This point takes us to the second of the NACCCE definitions.

Imaginative activity is purposeful

To undertake generative thought is not simply to daydream! Creativity needs to be applied to a purpose, and should result in an outcome. We know that creativity involves risk-taking, and not all creative endeavours will be earth-shattering but, nonetheless, they are original and creative for the student involved, and can be treated accordingly. Purposeful activity means there is some point to what is going on, and this can take a variety of forms.

Generate something original

It follows from our discussions of the work of Margaret Boden that originality is to be found in P-creative acts that students undertake. This means that originality can be thought of as being relative, rather than absolute. The implications of this for the teacher are that original work can be original for the students concerned, but maybe not original compared with what others have done. This does not mean that the students should feel in any way diminished by taking routes which others have taken before them, but that their creativity should be celebrated. It involves non-linear thinking to solve problems, and this can be found in many curriculum areas.

Outcome of Value

The NACCCE report has this to say about generating creative outcomes which are of value:

> We described imaginative activity as a generative mode of thought; creativity involves a second and reciprocal mode of thought: an evaluative mode. Originality at some level is essential in all creative work, but it is never enough. Original ideas may be irrelevant to the purpose in hand. They may be bizarre, or faulty. The outcome of imaginative activity can only be called creative if it is of value in relation to the task at hand. 'Value' here is a judgement of some property of the outcome related to the purpose. There are many possible judgements according to the area of activity: effective, useful, enjoyable, satisfying, valid, tenable. The criteria of value vary according to the field of activity in question.
>
> (NACCCE 1999: 33)

This is an important part of the creative process, it is about knowing whether the object provided fits the requirements. After all, if in a music lesson a creative response is required, perhaps in the form of a song, then the students need to know that it would not be appropriate to design and make a table! The outcome needs to bear some relation to the objectives of the task set.

Creativity in schools

Creativity is valued in society generally:

> Creativity is good for the economy and therefore for society. It is good for individuals who are more fulfilled when creative and who do not need to be Einstein to manifest creativity.
>
> (Craft 2003: 115)

In the National Curriculum creativity is also felt to be important:

> Creative activity is essential for the future wellbeing of society and the economy. It can unlock the potential of individuals and communities to solve personal, local and global problems. Creativity is possible in every area of human activity – from the cutting edge of human endeavour to ordinary aspects of our daily life.
>
> (QCA Curriculum Dimensions website n.d.)

Creativity appears in the value statements of many National Curriculum subjects, not just the ones where you might expect it. Here are some examples:

Maths:
Mathematics is a creative discipline.

Science:
The study of science fires pupils' curiosity about phenomena in the world around them and offers opportunities to find explanations. It engages learners at many levels, linking direct practical experience with scientific ideas. Experimentation and modelling are used to develop and evaluate explanations, encouraging critical and creative thought.

History:
History fires pupils' curiosity and imagination, moving and inspiring them with the dilemmas, choices and beliefs of people in the past.

Modern Foreign Languages:
Learning languages gives pupils opportunities to develop their listening, speaking, reading and writing skills and to express themselves with increasing confidence, independence and creativity.

All of these subjects feel creativity is important enough to warrant inclusion, and yet none might be considered to be ones which have an axiomatic association with creative processes.

Critical Thinking and Personal Learning and Thinking Skills

Thinking skills figure significantly in two National Curriculum domains. These are the cross-curricular dimensions, described above, and that of personal learning and thinking skills (PLTS). The similarities are such that it is worth considering them together for our discussions of cross-curricular learning.

In the case of the PLTS, the framework consists of six groups:

- independent inquirers
- creative thinkers
- reflective learners
- team workers
- self-managers
- effective participants

These are important areas of concern, and will be addressed as we look in more detail at specific aspects or cross-curricular learning.

Reflective task

Developing thinking might be thought of as being something that teachers will want to do automatically with their students. But what does it mean to want to have students who are independent inquirers, or reflective learners?

Are these skills?

If so, do you teach them?

Or do you expect students to somehow acquire them otherwise?

What does thinking mean anyway?

... and how do you teach it?

These are complex questions indeed! The way we shall set about addressing them is to consider what a taught curriculum for thinking might look like, and then use this as a way of considering how we can develop these ideas.

There is a probably apocryphal story about a lost motorist stopping in a strange town and asking a local inhabitant directions to nearby village, 'If I were going there, I wouldn't start from here' being the somewhat bewildering reply that they received! This is rather like the task we are engaged upon here. Instead of asking how we can teach thinking in schools, bearing in mind where we are now, how would it be if we were somewhere else, with a blank sheet of paper, and starting afresh? How would we foster teaching and learning for thinking?

> ## Practical task
>
> Have a go at answering this yourself. Think of two things you might do to developing thinking skills in students, without the constraints of your current situation.

Many answers teachers provide to this tend to involve two things:

- Active learning
- Problem solving

Maybe yours did too? Many see active learning as being key to developing thinking skills amongst our learners. Indeed, as brain-based research becomes more developed we are finding out that active learning is most likely to be the primary way we find out about, and engage with the world around us:

> The brain grows and increases, and intelligence increases, through being used. Strengthening brainpower, which is physiologically rooted in stimulating and reinforcing the synapses, strengthens learning. The brain loves to learn. Further, the brain is not a passive store of information; it thrives on activity, and actively seeks out information from the environment in order to learn – that is, it is proactive. There are more neural connections from the brain to the ear than from the ear to the brain, and some 10 per cent of the fibres in the optic nerve go 'the wrong way'. The brain, through sense organs, does not passively receive information, it deliberately goes fishing for it.
>
> (Cohen *et al.* 2004: 173)

Problem solving is often how active learning can be enacted. This can range from divergent thinking tasks, like demonstrating five different uses for a pebble; via the practical, such as how can we make better use of, or cut down on, waste paper in school, or how can we cut down on our carbon footprint at school; to specific, such as how can we use a set of specific materials to cross the school hall without touching the floor. These are useful activities to undertake, and go some way towards addressing concerns that education can be too involved in learning and recall,

> Creative problem solving is needed to make up for the shortcomings in our basic education where there has been an emphasis on the use of our mind for storing information instead of developing its power for producing new ideas and turning these into reality. Our productivity will be enhanced when we use our brain to question, explore, invent, discover and create – in other words, employ creative thinking. Through creative problem solving, we generate new ideas and innovative solutions for a given need or problem. These ideas will be more efficient and often of much higher quality. Creative problem solving gives balance to our thinking since it integrates analytical and imaginative thinking. Intuitive and interpersonal thinking are

as important as critical and structured thinking for achieving the best results. Thus, creative thinking skills are needed to help people accept and cope with change.

(Proctor 2005: 18)

Cross-curricular learning is needed for these to flourish. As the curriculum mapping discussion above revealed, a lot of single subject learning is focused on the assessment-driven model, whereby high-stakes summative assessment at the end point of a course drives the content to a considerable extent.

Summary

This chapter has introduced a number of ideas. It began by asking questions of knowledge, and what our understandings of curriculum entail. We have considered how the National Curriculum in the UK originally came into being as a series of separate subject areas. We then moved to a consideration of pedagogy, and of the important notion that teaching is not a one-to-one mapping onto learning. The cross-curricular dimensions of the National Curriculum have been discussed, and their importance as topics which exist outside, yet across subjects, was considered.

One of the key focuses for discussion has been the idea of a curriculum map, and establishing the range and scope of learning which is already taking place in schools, yet very often without all the threads being drawn together in a formal and logical fashion. Lave and Wenger's (1991) notion of the teaching curriculum being separate from learning curriculum was also discussed here. The nature of the cross-curricular learning which is planned for in the 14-19 diplomas was discussed, as was the thematic areas which are employed there. The linked notions of curriculum and assessment were introduced with key distinctions being drawn between two models of planning, curriculum led, and assessment led.

The key area of creativity, which will be a major informant to many aspects of this book was explored. The significant work of Boden (1990), where acts of P-creativity which allow the creative utterances of all pupils to be considered as being valid was outlined. PLTS and thinking skills were examined, and the role which they can play in cross-curricular learning introduced. Finally, we examined notions of identity and self, both from the perspectives of the students, and of the teacher.

Professional Standards

Part of the process of reflection which this book champions is that of making oneself accountable to processes of professional development. For those readers undertaking initial teacher education, this would include reflecting on the Q Standards regularly and building your evidence base that demonstrates your effective meeting of them. For those readers already working as teachers, there will be strategies of performance appraisal and review, which often involve these same standards, and require you to set targets and monitor your process through reflective cycles.

To assist with these processes, each chapter in this book, and the accompanying titles within the series, has considered how the text and activities within it have helped the reader meet the Q Standards for ITT, and the C Standards for those already in service. A summary of the application of these standards to the chapter follows. We trust that you will find this a helpful way of applying your work in reading the chapters (and your completion of any of the activities within them) to your wider professional development.

Meeting the Standards

This chapter will help you meet the following Q standards:
Q6, Q7, Q8, Q14, Q18

Professional Standards for Teachers

This chapter will help you meet the following core standards:
C6, C7, C8, C10, C15

Notes:

1 Thanks to Simon Spencer of Birmingham City University for this.

Artistic principles and purposes for cross-curricular teaching and learning

Key objectives

In this chapter we shall be looking at the many ways in which artistic principles for cross-curricular teaching and learning impact upon each other. By the end of this chapter you will have:

- Thought about different ways in which learning is organised in schools.

- Looked at the work of the highly influential Project Zero group, based at Harvard University, and at the work of teachers in Reggio Emilia in Italy.

- Started to think about skills and concepts, and of the part they play in the arts.

- Considered the relative importance of subjects within a cross-curricular teaching and learning programme.

- Reflected on what there is to learn in the arts – art-form specific and more generally.

- Considered what is involved in the creativity and creative processes.

- Thought about the role of qualitative judgements in the arts.

Ways of organising learning revisited

In Chapter 1 we considered ways of organising learning, and thought about how the perspective of the place of assessment can be a driving force in this. Let us now develop this argument, and think of other ways in which learning can be structured.

In the UK, and elsewhere, we have seen how the notion of a National Curriculum acts as a container for knowledge. But this is not the only way in which learning can be organised. Bernstein refers to two types of curricular organisation, 'collection' and 'integrated':

> ... if the contents are clearly bounded and insulated from each other, I shall call such a curriculum a collection type. Here the learner has to collect a group of favoured contents in order to satisfy some criteria of evaluation ... I want to juxtapose against

the collection type, a curriculum where the various contents stand in open relation to each other. I shall call such a curriculum an integrated type.

(Bernstein 1971: 49)

This binary formulation, although some years old now, still retains relevance in terms of the ways in which many schools conceptualise and organise learning experiences. Substitute 'assessment' for Bernstein's 'criteria of evaluation', and it becomes clear that, in a number of instances, it is assessment that drives programmes of study, which in turn become the curriculum.

Subject-based learning

We also saw in Chapter 1 that organising teaching and learning solely around the requirements of individual subject-based strands can be problematic. However, from a pragmatic perspective, structuring the curriculum in terms of delivering separate subjects can be seen to have a number of points in its favour:

From the conventional stand point, students learn subject matter. They and their teachers conceive of the educational task as committing to memory large numbers of facts, formulas and figures. Fixed in textbooks, such facts are taken as uncontroversial, their mastery valued as a sign of cultural literacy.

(Mansilla and Gardner 2009: 97–8)

This is teaching and learning conceived of at its simplest. It is teaching as telling, and learning as remembering. It is industrial, conveyor-belt style education; it maximises input compared with output, and:

there is an appealing sense of efficiency in subject matter teaching—large quantities of information can be rapidly presented to students and easily tested at scale.

(Mansilla and Gardner 2009: 99)

The authors of the publication from which these quotations were taken, Veronica Boix Mansilla and Howard Gardner, are both significant figures in Project Zero, based at the Harvard Graduate School of Education. Project Zero's mission is to 'understand and enhance learning, thinking, and creativity in the arts, as well as humanistic and scientific disciplines, at the individual and institutional levels' (Project Zero 2010). One of the key pieces of work that Project Zero produced was the *arts propel* work. In this Howard Gardner and the team looked into the ways in which learning took place across the arts:

we decided to look at three kinds of competences; PRODUCTION (composing or performing music; painting or drawing; engaging in imaginative or creative writing); PERCEPTION (effecting distinctions or discriminations within an artform, "thinking" artistically); REFLECTION (stepping back from one's own perceptions or productions, or those of other artists, and seeking to understand the goals, methods, difficulties, and effects achieved). PROPEL captures [this] acronymically

(Gardner 2006: 105)

These are themes which are useful to have as starting points for learning involving the arts, and many educational programmes have been constructed using materials from the *arts propel* work. Indeed, Project Zero itself is one of the most important informants on current thinking concerning education and the arts, and we shall be investigating research from its key figures on a number of occasions in this book.

What is also useful to note here is that the Project Zero approach takes us forward in our thinking about learning from perspectives other than the traditional subject-based approaches. Another arena in which the single-subject modality has been significantly challenged is that of the Reggio Emilia approach to early years education in Italy, and it is to that which we now turn.

Reggio Emilia

Reggio Emilia is a city in northern Italy, and it was there, and in the surrounding towns and villages, that a radical education style developed out of the ruins of the Second World War. It has continued to this day, inspiring teachers around the world with its focus on the development of children. What happens in this way of working is that:

> In Reggio, teachers and children build their knowledge, understanding and skills together – they are co-constructors of knowledge. The teachers see the value in building their curriculum framework around the interests of the children and the questions and ideas they present. Whilst the adults are careful to recognise individual learning styles, individual needs and forms of expression, they acknowledge group learning as highly important in their approach.
>
> (Thornton and Brunton 2007: 71)

This places a very different emphasis from a teaching-as-telling methodology in the ways in which teaching and learning are undertaken. If children are seen as co-constructors of knowledge, then the transmission model of education, where the teacher holds the knowledge and their role is to pass it on to the pupils, is no longer appropriate. The notion of co-construction of learning has ramifications for the ways in which we shall be viewing knowledge in cross-curricular learning, especially in project-based approaches. Indeed, the very notion of learning projects lies at the heart of work in Reggio Emilia:

> It is a collection of schools for young children in which each child's intellectual, emotional, social, and moral potentials are carefully cultivated and guided. The principal educational vehicle involves youngsters in long-term engrossing projects
>
> (Gardner 1998: xvi)

Also relevant for our purposes are the roles which are played by creativity and creative thinking in the Reggio approach:

- In Reggio creativity is at the heart of all learning experiences for young children. It is not tied to any particular area of the curriculum, but instead is a way of thinking, knowing and making choices and can be demonstrated in any aspect of learning. The Reggio Approach encourages the development of children's creativity by providing:
- open ended resources;
- a rich variety of experiences;
- space to explore materials;
- time to develop ideas;
- freedom to solve problems and try things out;
- the opportunity to learn skills;
- adults as role models of creativity.

(Thornton and Brunton 2007: 24)

The Reggio approach has been signally influential in early years education around the world. The practices it espouses, of creativity, of learning based on the interests of the children, and of children and adults working alongside each other, have had repercussions across many other areas of schooling too.

The very different work of Project Zero and Reggio Emilia both involve creativity, and creativity is going to be a major contributor to the arts when involved in cross-curricular teaching and learning, and so it is to a consideration of the role of the arts in cross-curricular learning that we now turn.

What is the role of the arts in cross-curricular teaching and learning?

Cross-curricular teaching and learning in the current educational context is likely to be interpreted in a variety of ways in different schools and other learning arenas. What all of these are likely to share are competing ideologies of different subject areas, the notion of perceived prestige of subjects, and the domain-defined specificity of the teacher's role. In order to think about what is specific about the arts, and the contribution the arts can bring to cross-curricular learning, we need to bear these points in mind. In a consideration of the role of the arts, a useful starting point is provided by Russell and Zembylas (2007), who ask an important question:

does arts integration require that that arts be defined as *disciplines* – an idea that emphasizes the intrinsic values of art in education, - or simply as "handmaidens" – an idea that focuses on the instrumental values of arts in education?

(Russell and Zembylas 2007: 288)

These are important distinctions. If arts are considered as disciplines, then there are contingent reasons to treat them as such. If, however, they are treated as 'handmaidens' then the corollary of this is that they become subservient to the need of others. Examples of the subservient nature of the arts in cross-curricular teaching and learning are readily to be found when projects tokenistically add painting a picture and singing a song to the real substance of cross-curricular learning which is taking place elsewhere. Artistic principles do not need to be discarded for true cross-curricular learning to occur. To counter this problem, Russell and Zembylas go on to observe:

> if we stop thinking in dualisms and move beyond the *either* (disciplines)/*or* (handmaidens) dichotomy, we may begin to examine arts integration on a totally different level of thinking – that is as multi-layered and symbiotic with other learning.
>
> (Russell and Zembylas 2007: 288)

This is the premise we shall want to move to centre-stage in our deliberations on cross-curricular learning. The notion of being 'multi-layered and symbiotic' is a key one in terms of thinking, planning and enacting cross-curricular learning, and we shall explore what this means in more detail in subsequent sections of this book.

Reflective task

Using Russell and Zembylas's (2007) notion of *disciplines* and *handmaidens*, are you able to think of any cross-curricular projects which you have been involved with, however peripherally, where these classifications could be used to apply to any aspects of learning which you saw taking place?

If we take heed of the warnings of Russell and Zembylas, and move beyond a simple dichotomy, then a more complex taxonomy of the ways in which the arts interface with the curriculum can be seen to have been provided by Liora Bresler (1995). In this she posits four styles of interactional modalities which the arts can have with the curriculum. These are:

1. The Subservient Approach

2. The Co-equal, Cognitive Integration Style

3. The Affective Style

4. The Social Integration Style

She provides this brief overview of each of the styles:

> In the first, the subservient style, the arts serve the basic academic curriculum in its contents, pedagogies, and structures. The second, the co-equal style, brings in the arts as an equal partner, integrating the curriculum with arts-specific contents, skills, expressions, and modes of thinking. The third, the affective integration style, emphasizes feelings evoked by and attitudes towards art, as well as student-centered learning and initiative, and it incorporates ideals of creativity and self-expression that

teachers and principals acknowledge are not served by the academic curriculum. The fourth style emphasizes the social function of the school and its role as a community.

(Bresler 1995: 34)

It is worthwhile giving some consideration to the ways in which these can operate in cross-curricular projects.

The arts as subservient

The notion of the arts as subservient relates very closely to the 'handmaidens' notion considered above. There are many stories of arts teachers being involved peripherally in planning and enacting cross-curricular learning experiences, often in such projects the involvement of the arts would be to 'prettify' the results from other subjects, so that, as we observed above, the students paint a picture, do a playlet or dance, or sing a song about it. None of these automatically involve arts learning experiences as valuable or integral to processes of active learning in and through the arts.

The co-equal, cognitive integration style

Teachers adopting the cognitive integration style often encouraged active perception and critical reflection on the technical and formal qualities of a project. In contrast to the subservient approach, the exploration included higher-order cognitive skills as well as aesthetic qualities.

(Bresler 1995: 35)

In the co-equal cognitive integration style, learning in and through the arts is placed on a similar footing to other curriculum areas. To work in this way will require significant input both at the planning and enactment stages from arts teachers. In many ways this style is the most appropriate to cross-curricular arts learning in terms of the ways in which knowing in and through the arts is treated.

The affective style

Bresler describes this as having two subcategories, change of mood, and creativity. With regard to change of mood, this involves such ideas as playing calm classical music whilst students do maths activities. Creative aspects were noted especially during integrated cross-curricular learning activities, where the opportunity existed for students to be involved in self-expression. This style could be viewed as being complementary to the curriculum, in that it provided for aspects which were deemed to be missing from it. However, arts teachers and practitioners are likely to want to argue for the unique role of the arts as having meaning in their own right.

The social integration style

Here, Bresler observes, '… the arts provided for the social functions of schooling' (Bresler 1995: 36). This is used as a way of integrating different aspects of cultural activity into the curriculum. Used unthinkingly this can lead to what Troyna pejoratively termed the 'Saris, Samosas and Steel bands' approach to multicultural education (Troyna and

Williams 1986). This notion was expanded upon by Gillborn, who observed that what it did was:

> to characterise the superficial multiculturalism that paraded exotic images of minority peoples and their 'cultures' while doing nothing to address the realities of racism and unequal power relations in the 'host' society
>
> (Gillborn 2000: 114)

This is the downside of the social integration style, the opposite is affirming and celebratory, with the arts acting as a catalyst for integration, and with learning and understanding built in to the work being done.

Implications

In Chapter 1 we considered ways in which cross-curricular learning can be conceptualised. One of the implications of Bresler's list of classifications is that it is appropriate to think about what the purpose of cross-curricular learning is when it is organised in schools. If the role of the arts is simply to act as 'filling', by including fripperies and decoration, then this will not serve learning in the arts well. Far more meaningful is for teaching and learning in the arts to be relevant and purposeful, and strengthened through collaboration, not diminished as a result. If in a cross-curricular learning unit the role of the arts is to paint a picture about the topic in hand, do a play, perform a dance, or sing a song about it, this is not mutually developmental in learning terms.

What is there to learn in the arts?

Having considered learning and knowledge in general terms, a key question to be asked of cross-curricular teaching and learning involving the arts is that of what there is to learn. This is quite a problematic question.

> ### Practical task
>
> Have a go at answering this question, 'What is there to learn in the arts'?
> What would you include, narrow it down to a few key points.

In thinking about answering this question, two immediate areas assume importance. These are:

1.   Domain specific knowledge

2.   More general learning

Items in the first group might include knowledge of style and technique, whereas the second group would include such matters as interpersonal skills, team work and cooperation.

Harland *et al.* (2005: 25) posited eleven broad outcomes from arts education interfaces. These are:

- Affective outcomes
- Artform knowledge, appreciation and skills
- Social and cultural knowledge
- Knowledge, skills and appreciation beyond the arts
- Thinking skills
- Developments in creativity
- Communication and expressive skills
- Personal development
- Social development
- Changes in attitudes towards and involvement in the artform
- Transfer beyond the artform

Although in many cases appertaining to individual artforms, these classifications are useful in helping us prepare for cross-curricular learning in the arts. Let us begin by considering the second item on the list, that of artform knowledge, appreciation and skills. This will be an instance of domain specific knowledge, and we will use it as an example of how artistic principles and purposes in cross-curricular teaching and learning.

Within this category, Harland *et al.* provide five elements of sub-classification. Again, these are a convenient means for framing thinking on learning. The sub-elements are:

- Artform knowledge
- Artform appreciation
- Artform skills and techniques
- Interpretive skills
- Ability to make aesthetic judgements

(Harland *et al.* 2005: 19)

This list is also helpful in decoding and making decisions about things which are to be learned. In aiming for Bresler's notion of the co-equal cognitive integration style, it is important for cross-curricular learning programmes to have domain specific knowledge, skills, and techniques addressed within them.

The order in which the subelements were presented above was that of the original authors, but in terms of our discussions in this chapter concerning learning, knowledge and skills, it is appropriate at this point to consider the first and third bullets together.

Knowledge and skills in domain specific arts contexts

Within any artform there are key knowledge items which learners will need to become acquainted with in order to become, in Lave and Wenger's (1991) terminologies, inducted into the community of practice of that artform.

Reflective task

If you are an arts teacher, what would you say are key knowledge items for your subject?

If you are not, what would you want your pupils to learn about your subject in a cross-curricular teaching and learning programme?

This is another complex topic area. To address it, let us take the key processes from the English National Curriculum orders for music and art, and compare what these two subjects require of their learners.

Table 2.1 Key processes at KS3 in National Curriculum art and music.[1]

	Art Key Stage 3	Music Key Stage 3
2.1	*Explore and create*	*Performing, composing and listening*
	Pupils should be able to:	**Pupils should be able to:**
a	develop ideas and intentions by working from first-hand observation, experience, inspiration, imagination and other sources	sing in solo or group contexts, developing vocal techniques and musical expression
b	investigate how to express and realise ideas using formal elements and the qualities of a range of media	perform with control of instrument-specific techniques and musical expression
c	make purposeful images and artefacts, selecting from a range of materials, techniques and processes	practise, rehearse and perform with awareness of different parts, the roles and contributions of different members of the group, the audience and venue
d	draw to express perception and invention, to communicate feelings, experiences and ideas, and for pleasure	create, develop and extend musical ideas by selecting and combining resources within musical structures, styles, genres and traditions
e	explore and develop ideas using sketchbooks, journals and other appropriate strategies.	improvise, explore and develop musical ideas when performing
f	–	listen with discrimination and internalise and recall sounds
g	–	identify the expressive use of musical elements, devices, tonalities and structures.

2.2	*Understand and evaluate*	*Reviewing and evaluating*
	Pupils should be able to:	**Pupils should be able to:**
a	use research and investigative skills appropriate to art, craft and design	analyse, review, evaluate and compare pieces of music
b	appreciate how codes and conventions are used to convey ideas and meanings in and between different cultures and contexts	identify conventions and contextual influences in music of different styles, genres and traditions
c	reflect on and evaluate their own and others' work, adapting and refining their own images and artefacts at all stages of the creative process	communicate ideas and feelings about music, using expressive language and musical vocabulary to justify their opinions
d	analyse, select and question critically, making reasoned choices when developing personal work	adapt their own musical ideas and refine and improve their own and others' work.
e	develop ideas and intentions when creating images and artefacts	–
f	organise and present their own material and information in appropriate forms.	–

Note

1 Some cells in the table are blank as the NC orders for the different subjects do not contain the same number of elements of content.

Table 2.1 shows the statutory requirements for the two subjects. What the requirements do not contain are specific items of knowledge content, rather they delineate the processes which students need to develop in order to make progress in their subject. This is a strength, in that it does not, say, require a detailed knowledge of Picasso's painting technique, or of blues singers of the 1920s. What this means is that the key processes can be used to plan learning in more general terms, aimed at including domain specific knowledge. To be more precise, let us consider item 2.1b from Table 2.1 for each of the subjects. This states that pupils should be able to :

Art: investigate how to express and realise ideas using formal elements and the qualities of a range of media

Music: perform with control of instrument-specific techniques and musical expression

To achieve this through a cross-curricular pedagogical approach, these processes will need to be addressed within the unique specificity of each artform, but in terms of commonality it is clear that both of these statements refer to aspects of *expression*. In planning teaching and learning, then, the notion of expression will need to be included in the programme which is devised. This can have broader implications than simply for art and music. Expression is important in dance, drama and English, and so planning for, and building in, provision for the development of expression will fulfil a variety of needs.

Skills too can be considered from multiple perspectives. Some skills are very much rooted in the specificity of the subject, so, for example, mark-making in art will involve a series of cognitive and sensory-motor skills, which will be different for pencil and brush. In music, instrument specific skills will also be important, such as knowing how to play an E chord on the guitar, for example. But skills of *realisation* can be seen to exist beyond single contexts. These can include skills of realisation in art and design, in drama, dance, and music. Again the important thing to do will be to involve provision for these to be nurtured and developed when planning cross-curricular learning projects.

Evaluative thinking in the arts

Evaluative thinking is one of the areas where the arts have something significant to contribute. In the work of Harland *et al.* (2005) the two areas of artform knowledge and skills which deal with evaluative thinking are those of *artform appreciation*, and the *ability to make aesthetic judgements*. The development of informed personal opinions is something that we know young people do, as this teacher observed:

> it's the easiest thing in the world to get kids to make aesthetic judgements. They do it all the time. The hardest thing in the world is to stop them. Oasis are better than Blur. Eastenders is better than Brookside. The question is how well they articulate it … and distinguish between the things which are personal and the things which are not necessarily universal or transcendental but are shared.
>
> (Raney and Hollands 2000: 21)

Aesthetic judgements, and their development, as the teacher cited by Raney and Hollands commented, are easily made, but justification for them is harder to establish and foster. In the arts, aesthetic judgements are linked to the person experiencing them, as well as being properties of the artform itself, as Roger Scruton observes:

> the significance of a truly meaningful work seems to grow with every encounter, so that these very words, tones, or lines become indelibly engraved in our perception, as the essence of the thing we love.
>
> (Scruton 1997: 375)

So as we engage with artforms it is possible the further and deeper meanings emerge for us. At school, students will listen to their favourite songs over and over again, they will read their favourite books, watch favourite films, play computer games, all with aesthetic appreciation. The role of education in aesthetics therefore needs to include a place for the individual in it. This produces a problem with regards to the approaches to aesthetic judgements and their function in education. This problem can probably best be thought of as a continuum, with education *in* cultural values at one end, and education *about* cultural values at the other.

Education in cultural values

Cultural values in arts education have been a contested arena for many years. The notion of education in cultural values frequently means that outsiders believe school students should learn about the great classics of Western civilisation. We looked at the introduction of the original National Curriculum in England in Chapter 1, and noted that there was a considerable furore. One aspect of this was with regard to the cultural values in which school students would be educated, with views such as this from Sir Rhodes Boyson, education minister in Margaret Thatcher's Conservative government, 'Schools are not holiday camps. They are there to keep a hereditary culture alive: great drama, religion and art' (Hymas 1991). The subject area that caused the one of greatest concerns was music, and opinions were publicly expressed about the cultural values that music should contain. For example,

> there is no excuse for allowing school music lessons to be infected with the prevailing values of the pop industry, which require nothing more musical from children than the ability to dip into their parents' purses to buy gormless videos of posturing idols
>
> (Morrison 1991)

But the production of National Curriculum music in a form which prioritised *knowing* music, rather than *knowing about* music, did not mean that the arguments were over. Indeed, it was not only politicians and the press who were concerned about values:

> Britain's unelected cultural commissar Dr Nicholas Tate, chief executive of the School Curriculum and Assessment Authority, called for 'educators' to impress on children that 'high' culture is good, profound and moral, whereas 'low' culture is base and worthless. Dr Tate is convinced that the threat posed by Blur to Schubert is so serious that unless we return to basics (in culture as well as morals) the core values on which Western civilisation was based will crumble away for good.
>
> (Wilkinson 1996)

This placing on the arts of the status of being guardians of the cultural values of Western civilisation was challenged:

> Today this is just not good enough. First in a multi-cultural society our culture is not just European. Second, a notion that high art is great and other forms of European music are not great is open to question. Third, the transmission of our cultural heritage, whatever we mean by this, is only one part of music education.
>
> (Mills 1991: 108)

And, tellingly, comparisons with some western civilisations which although concerned with cultural values, left a lot of other things to be desired.

> The idea of the arts as a cultural heritage in which children have to be initiated is not necessarily pernicious but it does need watching. The Third Reich in Germany was

in many ways rooted in European high culture and its leaders were certainly very conscious of the importance of the concept of heritage.

(Swanwick 1994: 169)

There are clear pitfalls in trying to educate students in cultural values, although this does not mean it should not be done. The issue of cultural relativism needs careful handling, especially as it can descend into a pointless 'mine is better than yours' argument. There are great masterworks which we would like our students to be aware of in the arts, but the 1950s version of 'cultural appreciation' lessons, containing filmstrips and gramophone records, is unlikely to work well with twenty-first century sensibilities. This does not mean that teachers and students should accept that all art products are equal, but that students should learn instead *about* cultural values, rather than be drilled in them.

Education about cultural values

The ability to make informed cultural judgements is an important part of the notion of aesthetic education found at the other end of the continuum. Here what is considered to be important is the notion of *informed critique*. This includes that which Harland *et al.* referred to as the *ability to make aesthetic judgements* which included the pupils' 'ability to make evaluative/critical judgements about the quality of works of art' (Harland *et al.* 2005: 19). Educating students in this fashion includes equipping them with both the analytical and linguistic tools necessary to be able to justify their opinions. Indeed, education about cultural values is probably best viewed as a process rather than a product. To undertake it properly involves discussion, justification and knowledge, and needs practice.

Values in the National Curriculum

In Table 2.1, key processes in the National Curriculum requirements for Key Stage 3 art and music were shown. If we return to this table, and extract key words from it, then this will serve two purposes. It will inform us as to the values espoused by these two subjects in the 2007 version of the National Curriculum, and it will enable us to consider key words which we can take forward for our consideration with regard to content in cross-curricular arts learning. Extracting key words, and grouping them together produces the result shown in Table 2.2.

This grouping and classification shows from a simple count that the art and music National Curriculum statements value *creation* in the artforms rather more than *knowledge* about them. The words for creation also outnumber significantly other facets of valued knowledge. But it is *evaluation* words which occupy the second tier in this straightforward counting exercise. What this seems to imply is that it is direct personal interaction with the arts which is valued, alongside developing ways of discussing opinions about them. This is a far cry from the opinions of the detractors of the National Curriculum outline above!

This way of extracting, looking at, and valorising key words is, of course, open to interpretation in a number of ways, and it may be more appropriate to present them in the form of a mind map or spider diagram rather than as a list, as this would allow interconnections to be shown.

Table 2.2 Key words in KS3 National Curriculum art and music, grouped thematically.

Creation words
> Create; Invention; Ideas
> Organise; Develop; Extend; Explore; Adapting; Improve; Refining
> Practise; Rehearse
> Selecting; Discrimination
> Expression
> Intentions
> Contextual; Styles; Genres; Traditions; Cultures and Contexts
> Purposeful

Communication words
> Perform; Communicate; Present

Affective words
> Feelings; Awareness; Perception

Evaluation words
> Justify; Opinions; Question Critically; Make reasoned choices
> Analyse; Compare
> Research; Investigate
> Evaluate; Appreciate
> Reflect

Acquired knowledge words
> Identify
> Vocabulary

It is possible that you may disagree with some of the categorisations we have made; again this is entirely open to interpretation, but the point is that the curriculum is not valuing specific knowledge *about* artforms. For example, no names are mentioned, it is not a list of important dead people, of the Mozart and Michelangelo variety. This is not great works of art as a museum (Goehr 1992), but is of education involving the arts as a practical, contemporary and living thing.

Practical task

Using the notion of key word extraction outlined above, choose your own subject or topic area, and another National Curriculum one. Extract the key words, and see if you can group them thematically.

If you prefer to, do this as a spider diagram or mind map.

If you are an art or music teacher, this task has been half done for you!

Using the key words as content

What is very helpful about the list of key words is that few, if any, of them are artform specific. If we broaden our thinking about the arts from art and music to include dance, drama, English, photography, media and so on, we can use the key words presented in Table 2.2 to form the basis for a consideration as to the type of activities and content themes which a cross-curricular teaching and learning programme could involve. It also involves thinking about the arts functioning in Bresler's notion of a co-equal cognitive integration style, and how they could both contribute to, and benefit from, such a teaching and learning programme. What is also of interest in looking at this list is how the words could readily fit with the components of the Project Zero *arts propel* acronym, namely production, perception and reflection. Another link here is that this also takes us to the notion of creativity, and the organisation of creative thinking in the arts, and so it is to the topic of creativity and creative processes which we now turn.

Stages in the creative process

Creativity was introduced in Chapter 1, and will figure like an *idée fixe* throughout this book. Creativity is one of the key processes which the arts bring to learning experiences, and within this it is useful to consider how it can be conceptualised in cross-curricular learning, and, indeed, why we would want it to figure in such processes.

In Chapter 1 creativity was discussed with reference to the NACCEE report as having two modes of thought, the *generative* and the *evaluative* (NACCCE 1999: 33). This was clearly the case in our consideration of the National Curriculum keywords with regard to art and music first shown in Table 2.2 above. Generative modes of creativity are ones which will produce new ideas, novel solutions and divergent approaches. However, these also need to be considered alongside evaluative modes of thinking, which will be employed in order to assess the worthwhile-ness, efficacy and quality of the ideas which are proposed. We shall continue to consider these two modalities in more detail as we progress through this book.

We need to address a frequently asked question with regard to creativity in the arts; this is the notion of creativity as *process* or *product*. This is no mere academic nicety. We saw in Chapter 1 how Margaret Boden (1990) wrote about P- and H- creativity, and of the ways in which these classifications could be used to describe the creative acts of students in classrooms. P- and H- creativity can be used as a categorisation of the creative acts which students undertake. What results from these creative acts, from the creative processes with which students are involved both within the classroom and beyond, are creative products. Here the distinction is important, and educators need to ask themselves a series of questions with regard to what is going on when creative acts are undertaken. These include:

Reflective questions for creative acts:

Am I prioritising the creative process?

… or am I prioritising creative products?

Does the process matter …

… or do I just want the pupils to come with something?

What will a high quality process entail?

What will a high quality product entail?

What is my role as teacher in this?

What happens if the process is good, but the product isn't?

What happens if the product is good, but the process was difficult?

What is novel/original/creative about this?

Who decides on the novelty/originality/creativity?

Wallas: Four stage model of creativity

Although written in 1926, the model of creativity proposed by Graham Wallas is often cited (Wallas 1926). It has many merits; it accounts for what we seem to observe in the creative process, the stages it delineates are clear and logical, and it is an elegant solution. In this model, Wallas outlines four stages of the creative process:

1.   Preparation

2.   Incubation

3.   Illumination

4.   Verification

The preparation stage does not just include getting ready to do something, it involves prior knowledge and experience too. During the incubation stages ideas are thought about, mulled over, and various ways of approaching the issue considered. Illumination can be thought of either as the 'Eureka moment', or as the point at which ideas finally drop into place. For some students this need not be a flash of inspiration, it can also occur as a result of working steadily at something. Wallas's final stage is that of verification. Here ideas are revised, revisited and generally made into a shape or form that can be considered as being fit for purpose. This is a very important stage, and involves a great deal of thought and application:

> One of the most demanding aspects of creative discipline is the revision process: artists and scientists clarify their condensed thoughts through the successive drafts (or

versions) of their work. Such efforts require the same active intelligence as generating novel ideas does.

(John-Steiner 1997: 75)

Indeed, for creativity in education, this is an important part of the learning about creative processes stage. Although creative ideas and solutions can emerge fully formed, it is common to have to work on and at them in order to produce something worthwhile. This is where nurturing creativity in education can help by focusing on process, and encourage students to revise and refine their ideas. Indeed, it is important for students to realise that revision and development of their creative ideas is an important and integral part of this process. Creative work with the students should, therefore, involve them in this revision, refining, and development stage, and the students need to come to appreciate that generating ideas is only one part in this complexity. We shall revisit this notion in Chapter 4 when we discuss editing.

Wallas's creativity model has a straightforwardness about it which makes it amenable to application in schools. As we think about creative processes in cross-curricular learning it will be apparent that it will be acting as an informant to these discussions.

Making qualitative judgements in the creative process

One of the implications of the Wallas model, and of the verification stage in particular, is that students need to come to understand what it is about their work that can be revised and, importantly, what judgements concerning the quality of their ideas that they need to make in order for this to happen. In many ways this has close linkages with assessment, especially formative assessment. As one of the early writers on formative assessment observed:

> The indispensable conditions for improvement are that the student comes to hold a concept of quality roughly similar to that held by the teacher, is able to monitor continuously the quality of what is being produced during the act of production itself, and has a repertoire of alternative moves or strategies from which to draw at any given point.

(Sadler 1989: 121)

This is important. It also makes very serious demands on the teachers, because they then need to have thought about what they might be looking for in terms of what the students can do. This does not mean that they have to have planned for all the possible responses that the students might come up with, but rather that they have considered what might be achievable, as well as being open to unforeseen outcomes, which are, after all, the essence of divergent thinking and creative responses. It is also appropriate for the teachers to be able to share aspects of qualitative outputs which they are looking for, especially as we know that teachers do not always do this, and that:

> There is considerable evidence that many students in classrooms do not understand what it is that teachers value in their work

(Wiliam 2000: 17)

But in order to do this, and, as Sadler observed, for the students to come 'to hold a concept of quality roughly similar to that held by the teacher', then the student has to be empowered with a critical vocabulary of qualitative expressions which serve the purpose of communication. Table 2.2 contains a number of evaluation terms and words which need to be enacted by the students concerned so that they are able to make reasoned judgements, and justify their own opinions. This means that programmes of cross-curricular learning need to include opportunities for learning this facility, as we cannot expect them to arise autochthonously, as it were, in other words, out of nothing. Learning opportunities need to be in place for this to happen.

Indeed, the area of critical judgements, and of pupils making them in terms of creative work in the arts is one which teachers will want to pursue anyway. To do this requires a programme of teaching and learning as much as any other content area of the curriculum. Many schools operationalise the expressing of critical judgements using a simplistic basis in the first instance, employing the well-known 'two stars and a wish' methodology. This acts as a thinking-frame, and entails students making evaluative comments about each others' work by first of all presenting two positive aspects of critique, before proffering suggestions for improvement. Whilst some secondary school teachers have observed that this has a primary school feel to it, nonetheless being positive first is helpful from both motivational and metacognitive perspectives. It is motivational because it prevents students assuming critique means to criticise in a negative sense, and it involves metacognition in that students are required to think about the nature of the qualitative responses they are giving.

From common ground to artform-specific principles

We have discussed creativity and thinking skills in general terms so far in this chapter. It is, however, inevitable that there will be certain skills and techniques which are artform-specific, and which students will need to acquire and participate in, in order to develop their capabilities in that domain. For example, these include mark-making skills in art, performance skills in drama, and instrument-specific skills in music. It is important that these distinctions are observed, and that students are given the opportunities to develop these skills. The purpose of cross-curricular work is not to substitute general skills for specific ones, but to develop commonalities which can be used as well as domain-specific skills. It is to the development and application of these ideas that we now turn our attention in the next chapter, as we consider the pedagogy and practice of cross-curricular teaching and learning within and beyond the arts.

Summary

This chapter has introduced many of the important themes of cross-curricular teaching and learning involving the arts which will reappear a number of times during the course of this book. The roles of creativity, and of the various stages, from generation to revision have been discussed, and the notion of creativity, and creative processes has been seen to be central to a consideration of the educational place of the arts. We have also begun to consider the role of evaluative statements, and of the ways in which pupils require education in the process of doing this.

Meeting the Standards

This chapter will help you meet the following Q standards:
Q6, Q7a, Q8, Q22, Q25B

Professional Standards for Teachers

This chapter will help you meet the following core standards:
C6, C7, C8, C15, C20, C29B, C39, C40

3

The pedagogy and practice of cross-curricular teaching and learning within and beyond the arts

Key objectives

In this chapter we will investigate pedagogies and practices of cross-curricular teaching and learning involving the arts, and think about the important issue of planning pedagogic approaches. By the end of this chapter you will have:

■ Thought about planning for cross-curricular teaching and learning.

■ Asked questions about planning for teaching and learning.

■ Thought about what a pedagogy for cross-curricular teaching and learning in the arts entails.

■ Considered group learning, and the ways in which students are, and can be, grouped.

■ Reflected on different types of knowledge.

■ Thought about the inter-relationships between learning and knowledge.

■ Considered the difference between *learning* and *doing*.

■ Reflected on the role of learning theory.

■ Thought about the work of Vygotsky, and its relevance to teaching and learning in the arts.

■ Considered the role of Pedagogic Content Knowledge.

■ Considered the valorisation of knowledge, and the hierarchies which result.

■ Reflected on the importance of understanding in the arts.

Starting points – why cross-curricular?

Many schools have identified that there are issues which they need to address with their cohort of students, with their curriculum and with the way that they can maximise student learning experiences. In one school in Birmingham where this was the case, the head teacher was clear in his analysis:

The level of dislocation and non-engagement in school is high whether you measure it by behaviour, SATS, GCSE, school attendance. This is a school where children need to be more engaged with the curriculum. If you take on board the scale of literacy issues and language deficit and barriers to learning that are language and literacy related, then I think that that's another major starting point. The extent to which many Birmingham secondary schools with large EAL issues are used to a pattern of very low achievement against national averages at KS3 and a degree of catch-up at KS4, it's almost as if we accept that language deficit coming into a specialised curriculum is going to mean that there is a year or two of just floundering and struggling. Then I think the whole transition question, transition plus language deficit in the secondary curriculum, are all reasons why we've got to do something. The extent to which there is a casual or under-developed assent to ideas around multiple intelligence and diverse learning styles without people actually engaged rigorously or significantly in applying those things, those would be my starting points I think …

(Fautley *et al*. 2008: 13)

For these reasons the head and staff in this school adopted a cross-curricular approach to teaching and learning in Year 7, and this helped both smooth the transition from primary schools to Year 7, and develop learning in a broader sense for these pupils. This is an example of a situation-reactive implementation of cross-curricular learning and, in this instance, considerable time was spent on planning before the new curriculum was enacted. The concept of planning for teaching and learning is a key one, and we refer to it on a number of occasions throughout this book. Although we have thought about planning already in earlier chapters, it is worth revisiting, this time to ask some hard questions about the function and place of teaching and learning in cross-curricular programmes involving the arts.

Planning for cross-curricular learning

In Chapter 1 we considered the idea of planning for learning being either driven by assessment, or where assessment follows learning, and in Chapter 2 we started to look at what there is to learn in the arts. We can now visit these again, and begin to draw some of the threads together, in order to consider in more detail the nature and scope of planning for teaching and learning.

Let us begin with an area we started in chapter two, where we saw how it is much easier to plan for activity, for *doing,* than it is for learning.

Cross-curricular learning is not the same as cross-curricular activity! This is an important point to establish before arts subjects can become involved in putative cross-curricular learning activities. We do not want all cross-curricular learning involving the arts to take on the characteristics of what we saw in Chapter 2 as Bresler's notion of subservience. So, even before planning can begin, teachers of the arts should ask some hard questions. The first series of these questions are shown in Figure 3.1, which outlines them in flowchart form.

The most common question in Figure 3.1 is 'Why?', appearing at a number of turns in the flowchart. This is a key question for teachers to be asking! In many cases students

> ## Practical task
>
> Many schools require teachers to share learning outcomes with pupils at the start of a lesson. If you have to do this, as you share your learning outcomes in coming lessons, ask yourself if what you are sharing are really *learning* outcomes, or are they, in fact, *task* outcomes? Do they say, for instance, 'today we will learn…' or do they say 'today we will do…'?
>
> Are the learning outcomes you write in your lesson plans the same as the ones you share with the students, or do you simplify them? Do you, for example change your *learning* outcomes into *task* outcomes to make it simpler for the students? Does this matter?

will already be attuned to asking this question, 'Why are we doing this?' being frequently heard in the classroom; teachers can learn from this, and ask the same question! Indeed, there is an important point of curriculum design here, in that timetable time is so precious that any decision to include some aspect of learning means that many other aspects have to be excluded in order to make room for it. This involves making decisions with regards to priorities, and really thinking about which aspects warrant inclusion, and which can be dealt with elsewhere. This is a development of the curriculum mapping process we discussed in earlier chapters.

Figure 3.1 is structured to show artform-related questions mostly on the left hand side of the chart, and other more general areas on the right. Having asked, and, hopefully, answered the first questions, the next level of planning decision making involves a consideration of what aspects of the arts students will be learning. This cannot be overemphasised. Learning should take place, and this needs to be relevant arts learning. The question 'why' which follows this is an important one. Let us take some time to consider this one question in more detail.

What aspects of the arts will the student be learning?

Good question! In the United Kingdom, the National Curriculum determines to some extent the nature of what will be learned. As we have seen in earlier chapters, what it tends not to do in many cases is to dictate much by way of content. This is left by and large to individual schools to determine.

> ## Practical task
>
> What are the areas of content of the curriculum which you currently teach?
>
> Why are they there?
>
> Who decided?
>
> If you could replace one area with something else, what would it be?

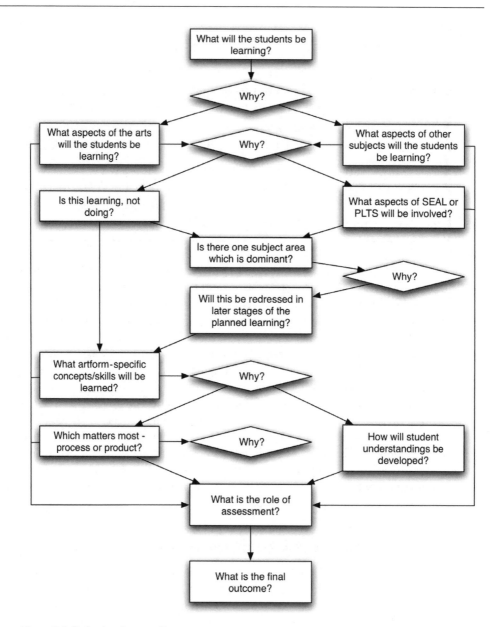

Figure 3.1 Early planning questions.

Kelly (2009) distinguishes between a number of ways of organising the curriculum. The way that the reflective task above asks you to consider he calls *the content model*. He contrasts this with *the objectives model*, where the curriculum is determined by statements of objectives, framed in terms of targets. This equates fairly closely with the ways in which we considered assessment as a driver of the curriculum in Chapter 1. However, what Kelly then goes on to say is that neither of these models are really adequate:

The simple fact that emerges from the whole of this discussion is that neither the content model nor the objectives model, nor even a combination of the two, can provide us with a template for the planning of a truly educational curriculum or one which is consonant with the underlying principles of a democratic society. In fact, and more seriously, the use of these models for the planning of the whole schooling system results in a curriculum which is quite inappropriate and which inhibits the attainment of education for all pupils.

(Kelly 2009: 86)

The reasons for this are that we need to separate out another idea we looked at earlier, Lave and Wenger's (1991) description of the differences between a teaching curriculum and a learning curriculum. A teaching curriculum can be systematic, but linearity is not always appropriate, especially where learning in the arts is involved. A learning curriculum, on the other hand, needs to have an element of reflexivity built into it, and this is where assessment *for* learning, which we shall consider in Chapter 6, has such an important role to play. What is most likely to be helpful is a view of learning which responds to the pupils in the classes concerned, not an idealised version of progression. Kelly calls this *curriculum as process and development* (Kelly 2009: 89), and it is a particularly apposite model for our discussions concerning cross-curricular learning from the standpoint of the arts.

Case study – curriculum as process – flags

Making links between subjects, and undertaking true cross-curricular learning where the arts are given prominence is an important aspect of what we are trying to achieve. An example of this is to be found in a cross-curricular learning programme based on the notion of 'flags'. Here creative potential is opened up via a number of the arts. Indeed, it is the *creative learning* potential of cross-curricular projects which can form one of their most powerful modes of expression. The notion of flags carries with it a number of ideas which can be deconstructed by the learners, and in this project students are able to think in a number of areas transcending boundaries between subjects. These include a number of what we might call 'big issue' questions, such as:

- What is a flag?
- What does it represent?
- What is a nation?
- Where do I belong?
- Can I have allegiance to more than one flag?
- What about my parents/grandparents?
- What should a nation stand for?
- What values would we want in a nation?
- What is a refugee?
- What should the role of young people be?
- What are rights?
- What are responsibilities?

- Do we need rules/laws?
- If so why?
- Who should decide?
- What does authority mean?
- What does 'freedom' mean?
- Does someone have to be in charge?
- Why?
- What does 'society' mean?
- What is my role in this society?
- What happens if I don't agree?
- What do we do with people who don't agree?
- What is repression?
- Why does it happen?

These questions can be explored in a number of ways, and the outworking of them can be found in a number of areas. For example, one way this can be investigated concerns a variation on William Golding's novel *Lord of the Flies*. In this scenario, the students are somehow transported to an otherwise uninhabited island. Creative responses to this scenario need not be captured solely in single subject-based artforms, but can certainly include the following:

Visual:
- Design fantasy landscapes
- Construct fantasy landscapes
- Design new flags
- Draw illustrations of journeying
- Make 3D images of difference
- Look at medieval maps of the 'here be dragons' variety
- Design their own maps accordingly ...
- ... with new fantastic people and animals contained therein
- Images of society

... and many more besides

Dramatic:
- Role plays of journeying
- Different forms of authority
- The notion of dissent
- The place of the individual
- The person who disagrees
- The idea of being right
- Being alone in society

... and many more besides

Musical:
- Music for a journey
- Making a new musical language
- Music for ceremonies
- Music for the flag
- Music with a sense of place
- Music of dissent
- Composing for telling stories
- Creating music which represents a new order
- Personal feelings in creating music
- Music for nostalgia
- Songs of nationhood
- Songs of struggle
- Songs of repression
- Songs of yearnings for freedom

… and many more besides

Multimedia:
- Films of journeying
- Interviews with people who have journeyed
- Montage of personal experiences
- Representations of statelessness
- What is propaganda?
- Making a propaganda film
- Films of repression
- Films of liberation
- Personal narratives/video diaries

… and many more besides

The written word:
- Stories of journeys
- The travel diary
- The notion of the spirit of place
- Stories and poems which evoke a spirit of place
- Narratives of struggle
- The call of the wild
- Freedom and persecution
- Poems of dissent
- Tales of struggle
- The role of the folk-story
- Stories that bind people together

… and many more besides

It is clear from this outline that this unit of learning also encompasses work which involves geographical, historical, cultural, societal, moral and religious aspects of teaching and learning. Also involved is scientific knowledge, for example navigation, astronomy, food and healthy living, including links to food technology; design technology, including how to build shelters, and, as the lists above reiterate, many more besides.

Pedagogy for 'flags'

There is clearly a lot of learning taking place in the 'flags' project. There are important moral and political views which this work addresses, and it would be inappropriate to shoehorn it into a linear sequence. What is important for this and similar projects, is that pedagogy does not and should not necessarily mean linearity of teaching. There are key items which the pupils should be learning, but this does not mean that all classes have to be *taught* them in the same order. This does not mean that cross-curricular teaching and learning programmes should be treated as a freeform do-what-you-like event, far from it. All of the teachers involved in delivering cross-curricular learning programmes of the sort we advocate are insistent that it requires more, not less planning than the more normal single-subject methodology. This is because for some of the time the teacher will not be delivering, but facilitating, not giving information, but enabling the students to become co-constructors of their own learning. To do this requires a bigger view of the overall teaching and learning picture, and an understanding of the stages which will be passed through en route. A diagrammatic representation of this is shown in Figure 3.2.

The right hand side of Figure 3.2 shows the more traditionally planned single subject linear route through a learning programme, the left hand side shows the more complex route that an extended learning programme can involve. The differences between the two take us back to earlier chapters, where we discussed Lave and Wenger's (1991) notion of a *teaching curriculum* as opposed to a *learning curriculum*. We noted in the former, teaching is the main focus of activity, whereas in the latter the main focus is on learning. Figure 3.2 clearly shows this. The right hand side is planned to suit the teacher, whereas in the model espoused on the left hand side, it is the learners themselves who govern the move from one learning item to the next. If we think of the notion of the curriculum we also introduced in Chapter 1, what is happening here is that on the left hand side the teacher needs a grasp of the overall route plan, whereas on the right hand side they are more concerned with the stages in-between. This is why planning for cross-curricular teaching and learning programmes which involve reacting to students' wants and needs can be more demanding. However, although they demand more of the teacher, they can also be significantly more rewarding for both teacher and students:

> it's made me realise that there's a lot more that you can do to make your lessons more interesting, more accessible, just more appropriate to the pupils and it's made me really think about that and, you know, I'm trying to influence my normal teaching too
>
> (Fautley *et al*. 2008: 40)

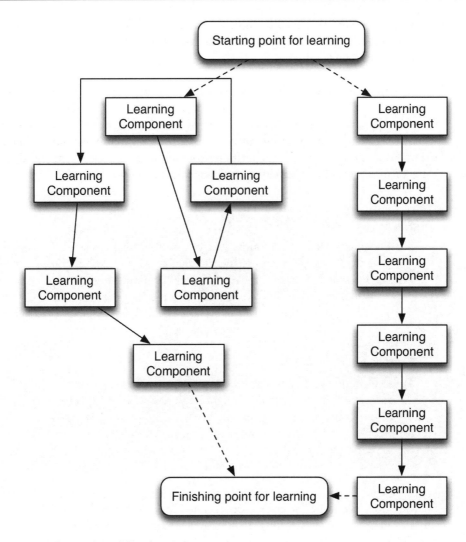

Figure 3.2 Routes through learning.

One of the implications of teaching and learning in this fashion is that for the teacher it involves being reactive, in the way that historically good teaching has always been, rather than prescriptive, in the sense that 'it's lesson 14 of the programme, we must study coastal erosion today'. This does not mean that the topic of coastal erosion will not be covered, but that it will become appropriate to be covered when the learners are ready. A science teacher I interviewed put it like this:

> The learning is driving what we are doing. If I say, 'right we are going to learn how to save the world', they will say, 'right then teach us about global warming'. So they actually tell me what to teach. I had some students today who said, 'we learnt about leaves today so could we look at some under microscopes?' So tomorrow we're going to look at some under microscopes. They get to drive the teaching and learning a lot

more than with traditional teaching. If a kid said, 'can we look at a leaf under the microscope?', the teacher would normally say, 'well, if we have time, but actually we need to be ready for this test'.

Here, as in many current educational issues, the answers always seems to devolve to assessment. This will be covered in more detail in Chapter 6, but for the moment the important thing to note from this teacher talking is the importance of the learners 'driving what we are doing'. Empowering learners does not mean disempowering teachers, quite the opposite. To work in a pedagogic framework of this nature the teacher needs to have a 'big picture' view of the curriculum, not an atomistic linear view.

Story

I was having my hair cut recently. As barbers do, I was asked what my job was. Upon saying I worked in teacher training the barber promptly told me stories of his education, and then made the observation that it must be easy being a teacher, because you only had to be two pages ahead in the textbook from the children to teach anything! I asked him how he'd like his children taught by a teacher like that, and he was rightly angry at the prospect.

Reflection:

Folk views of being a teacher such as this may be the stuff of saloon-bar conversation, but how true they might be now is doubtful. In the cases we are discussing, it should be clear that the teacher needs a thorough overview of the learning involved, as it is non-linear, and pupil driven. Being two pages ahead of the learners will not be possible!

So what does pedagogy for cross-curricular teaching and learning entail? And does it differ from single-subject teaching? In the flags learning, a team of teachers were deployed, all working with the same group of learners for protracted periods of time. Within the team were a range of specialisms, but all the teachers taught across the full range of subjects. In this sense the pedagogy was akin to that of the primary school, where a single class teacher has responsibility for the whole range of the curriculum. Indeed, as an integral component of cross-curricular working, the secondary school in this instance had employed a primary school practitioner to advise and shape the way that cross-curricular teaching and learning could be facilitated in the school (Fautley *et al.* in press).

Pedagogy revisited

In the accompanying overview book in this series (Savage 2011), Robin Alexander's notion of pedagogy was discussed, and it is worthwhile thinking about this here, and considering it in the light of cross-curricular learning and teaching in the arts. Alexander defined pedagogy as being:

the act of teaching together with its attendant discourse. It is what one needs to know, and the skills one needs to command, in order to make and justify the many different kinds of decisions of which teaching is constituted.

(Alexander 2004: 11)

This gives rise to the twin notions discussed in the overview book, of *pedagogy as act*, and *pedagogy as discourse*.

Pedagogy as discourse is conceived around three levels of ideas that relate to the classroom, the system (including policies that determine the system) and wider aspects of society and culture. All of these, Alexander asserts, 'enable, formalise and locate the act of teaching' (ibid). ... These discursive components of pedagogy translate into a model of 'pedagogy as act' that contains three main categories: frame, act and form.

(Savage 2011: 47)

These ideas are important to our understanding of what is entailed in pedagogy, and the way these are operationalised in the day to day activity of the classroom. As Alexander goes on to observe:

The core acts of teaching (task, activity, interaction and assessment) are framed by space, pupil organisation, time and curriculum, and by routines, rules and rituals. They are given form and are bounded temporally and conceptually by the lesson or teaching session.

(Alexander 2004: 12)

This gives us a helpful list of pedagogic components. This list is:

Core acts	Framing
task	space
activity	pupil organisation
interaction	time
assessment	curriculum
	routines
	rules
	rituals

Reflective task

How many of the items on this list are you in control of in your lessons?

How many are set by forces beyond your control?

If you wanted to change any of these, where would you begin?

Are there any in your context which are not amenable to questioning? If so, which, and why?

Undertaking cross-curricular teaching and learning is likely to call a number, if not all, of these items into question. Let us consider what this means for each of these now, with the exception of assessment, which is dealt with separately in Chapter 6.

Core acts

In traditional single-subject teaching there are three sources for tasks and activity based components, these are:

i)   National Curriculum prescriptions;

ii)   teacher preferences; and

iii)   subject-specific conventionality.

These all form competing pressures on tasks. Examining learning again from an integrated perspective, as in the example of the flags project above, forces this issue into the open.

National Curriculum prescriptions concerning tasks are few and far between in the arts. Indeed, as we have seen previously, there is little by way of specificity here: learning is conceptualised in terms of key processes. Teacher preferences are clearly a matter for individual concerns, and as we saw in Chapter 1, these can be placed into context where different topics are appropriate for different school locales, so learning can be made relevant for differing school populations. Subject-specific conventionality, on the other hand, often forms what Bruner (1996) referred to as a 'folk pedagogy', where content is included in the curriculum often as a sort of received wisdom, because all other subject teachers do it! Thus, for example most KS3 music curricula include a unit on the blues. In a similar fashion, with regard to art and design, John Steers noted that:

> the history of art education in schools is littered with examples of 'school art'. It is easy to recall a sequence of once fashionable and ubiquitous images: monotone drawings of Che Guevara; work dependent on the Sunday newspaper colour supplements; studies of sections of vegetables and fruit; baseball boots and trainers; images from 'in' record sleeves; crushed Coca-Cola cans; rubber plants; reflections in stainless steel kitchen utensils – to that long-running all-time favourite, the sliced pepper. What these 'school art' exercises have in common is their almost total lack of any relationship to contemporary art and design activity beyond the school art room.
>
> (Steers 2004: 27)

Considered from a cross-curricular perspective, the tasks and activities for learning that arise from the flags project, for example, are of a totally different order. This presents opportunities, but also challenges. It is an opportunity to move away from received wisdom as far as the curriculum is concerned, but it is also a challenge, in that there can seem to be an element of risk, as the teacher is not the primary agent of curricular momentum, but is reacting to the wants and needs of the pupils.

Classroom Interactions

Interactions in the classroom can occur between the teacher and the pupils, and between the pupils themselves. One of the features of cross-curricular teaching and learning is that it can often move away from teacher directed learning, and enable greater interaction between the pupils themselves. It can also, as the quotation from the science teacher earlier in this chapter shows, enable the pupils to make direct requests of the teacher, in that case, 'teach us about global warming'. But pupils can also ask questions of the teacher. Here is a deputy head speaking to me:

> I want to see students asking questions in lesson. If they are asking questions, they are thinking, if they are thinking, they are learning. I want to see good questions from the teacher. Not low level recall questions, they're tedious, but good questions to get the children thinking. I observed one of my teachers recently, and they asked me to focus on questioning. So I said to them, 'I counted your questions in this lesson, you asked 49 questions altogether, 37 of them were answered by a single word. What do you think of that?' That's powerful. We then thought about what sort of questions that the teacher could ask, and he found that very powerful, it's real evidence.

Practical task

How many questions do *you* ask that can be answered by a single word?

Do you know?

Why not pair up with a colleague and find out?

Interactions between pupils also matter. How pupils interact with each other in lessons can affect their learning significantly. The ways in which pupils can, and do, learn from each other can make a real difference to their understandings too. This is a point we shall revisit later in this chapter, when we consider some of the theoretical implications of ways of viewing learning.

Framing

The framing aspects of pedagogy include a number of areas which potentially are beyond the remit of an individual teacher. For example, the available space is unlikely to be altered radically. But how the space is used is often amenable to alteration.

Reflective task

Do you have a classroom?

Why is it set up the way it is?

Do you have desks or tables?

How are they used?

How often do you change the arrangement of the furniture?

Thinking about the space that is at your disposal can produce some interesting results. Many classrooms have movable stackable tables, rather than heavy old desks, and these can be repositioned readily to allow students to move between them to facilitate different types of learning. Moving tables also allows for grouping of pupils to be undertaken in different ways for different types of learning, and this takes us to the next item on the list, pupil organisation.

Student organisation and grouping

> ## Reflective task
>
> How are pupils grouped for you?
>
> Do you have sets, streams, or mixed ability groups?
>
> Do you have a preference?
>
> If so, what, and why?

How pupils are organised in order for you to teach them is probably determined by the school, but how you organise them within your lesson is up to you. (Kutnick *et al.* 2005) investigated the ways in learners were grouped together in secondary school classrooms, and found some serious issues with what they saw:

> there was some indication that pupils' within-class seating may not promote classroom learning, for example: (1) while 20% of classroom tasks concern new (cognitive) knowledge, 57% of these tasks took place in whole class settings where the teacher dominated proceedings…; and (2) practice and revision tasks (19% of assigned tasks) were least likely to take place in an individual setting as pupils were rarely seated as individuals
>
> (Kutnick *et al.* 2005: 367)

The implications of this finding are quite significant, in that what Kutnick *et al.* are saying is that teachers have set up ways of learning where there could be an inherent tension between the way the pupils are grouped, and the sorts of learning that the teacher is trying to promote.

> ## Reflective task
>
> So, how do you group the pupils in your classes?
>
> Do you always use the same type of grouping?
>
> Do you vary this within and between classes?
>
> Do you have a rationale for the types of grouping you employ?

The ways in which pupils can be organised in groups differs between teachers, and between subjects. A useful overview of ways in which possible groupings can be put together, and strengths and weaknesses of each, is to be found in the National Strategy materials, a summary of which is to be found in Table 3.1.

Table 3.1 Benefits and limitations of different groupings.

Grouping	Benefits	Limitations	When to use
Friendship	Secure and unthreatening	Prone to consensus	When sharing and confidence building are priorities
Ability	Work can more easily be pitched at the optimum level of challenge	Visible in-class setting	When differentiation can only be achieved by task
Structured mix	Ensures a range of views	Reproduces the power relations in society	When diversity is required
Random selection	• Builds up pupils' experiences of different partners and views • Accepted by pupils as democratic	Can get awkward mixes and 'bad group chemistry'	• When pupils complain about who is allowed to sit with whom • When groups have become stale
Single sex	Socially more comfortable for some	Increases the gender divide	In contexts where one sex habitually loses out, e.g. competing to control the computer keyboard

Source: National Strategies 2006: 12–13.

What Table 3.1 shows is that the five possible ways in which pupil groupings can occur each have their own inherent advantages and disadvantages associated with them, and that it is likely to be a matter of personal preference by the teacher as to which of the methods is preferred.

We cannot assume a commonality of groupwork in all subjects of the curriculum. The ways in which pupils work together in the arts can be radically different from the way, say, in which they work together in science to undertake an experiment, in history to decode a primary source, or in geography to read a map. Each of these specific groupwork activities requires a certain type of pupil interaction. However, a challenge for teachers is teaching the groupwork skills they require, for the needs of the pupils. As Kutnick *et al.* observe, 'teachers in this study rarely provided support or training for group working skills' (Kutnick *et al.* 2005: 368). The implications of this are that groupwork is established without the pupils necessarily knowing the sorts of interaction or, possibly, the sorts of learning, which the teacher intends them to undertake. As a common methodology for groupwork to take place in secondary schools is friendship groups, 'it may be left to the power of friendship to provide the necessary circumstances for communication and support, allowing enhancement of cognitive activity' (ibid.). What this means for teachers is that friendship groups are often employed as a means of short-circuiting some of the interpersonal relationship issues that other groupings can create. Friendship groups 'were often stereotypical – legitimating gendered, ability and other preferences' (ibid.). In other words what the authors of this research found was that friendship groups were often made up of either all male or all female friends, who tended to be more or less the same in terms of their abilities.

Matters of curriculum we cover elsewhere in this book, and so the next items on Alexander's list to consider are routines, rules, and rituals, which we shall take together.

Routines, rules, and rituals

Every teacher tends to have certain ways they like things to be done. A common activity for trainee teachers to undertake is a pupil trail, where they follow a pupil around the school, and experience the full breadth of the curriculum as experienced by the pupils. Senior leadership teams often do this too, but the opportunity for other teachers to learn from this experience is less common, unfortunately.

Reflective task

Are there routines, rules, and rituals you have in your teaching?

Are you consciously aware of them?

Are there some which have arisen through your own custom and practice without you having given them much thought?

Try to see your classroom as if you were a stranger. What do you want done, by whom, and when? Then ask yourself why!

There is a certain rhythm to the school day, and to lessons within it. One of the challenges for cross-curricular learning is to break this structure, and move the pupils to a process of deep learning, where they are not simply undertaking regurgitatory activities, but are instead engaging with content and processes. Challenging routines can be a part of this, and it is to one such challenge that we look later this chapter when we investigate the notion of 'the Mantle of the Expert'.

From pedagogy to learning and knowledge

We have been looking at Alexander's conception of pedagogy so far in this chapter, but before we can proceed much further with thinking about this, we need to disentangle terminologies which apply to teaching from those which apply to learning.

Let us start by considering a fairly important question, namely, what is learning?

> **Reflective task**
>
> You will already have a view as to what learning is. Can you describe it, and say what sorts of things take place when you think about it?

Learning is an extraordinarily complex construct, and learning and knowledge are often considered as being interrelated, you learn knowledge, and the knowledge you have is because you have learned it! But is it that simple? To say you learn knowledge seems to be a very bland statement. It also seems to presuppose that all knowledge is more or less the same, and that it enters through a single experience called learning. To get at learning, therefore, we also need to think about knowledge.

> **Reflective task**
>
> Think about something you know.
>
> What is it, how do you know it, and how do you know you know it?

In undertaking this reflective task it is likely that the things you thought about here could vary considerably. Maybe it was a fact, for example, Bognor is by the seaside. Maybe it was a skill, like knowing how to ride a bike. Maybe it was a person, for instance 'I know my Aunt Sharon'. Maybe it was a mood, 'I know I like being happy'. Maybe it was a memory, 'I know I enjoyed my holiday in Scotland last year'. Possibly a food, 'I know mussels are my favourite dish'. Or maybe it was something else entirely! Whatever it was, it will be useful to deconstruct it, and try to grasp some of its complexities. For example, if you know how to ride a bike, is this a different type of knowledge from knowing that Paris is the capital of France? In cross-curricular teaching and learning, do these represent different knowledge types, and, if so, what sort of impact might this have? The branch of philosophy which deals with learning is epistemology. There are a number of complex arguments concerning epistemology, but for our purposes we are concerned with two key aspects, types of knowledge, and how people come by knowledge.

Types of knowledge

One of the primary distinctions between knowledge types is that between 'knowing that', and 'knowing how', a distinction often credited to Gilbert Ryle (1949). In the example given above, knowing how to ride a bicycle is an example of 'knowing how', and knowing that Paris is the capital of France is an example of 'knowing that'. Another way of thinking about the same split in knowledge types is provided by the labels 'declarative knowledge', and 'procedural knowledge', where declarative knowledge is, literally, knowledge which can be declared, in other words can be spoken out loud, whereas procedural knowledge is 'knowing how', knowing from the inside ways in which things are done. The example of riding a bike is apposite here. In declarative terms it is relatively straightforward to tell someone what to do: get on, pedal, steer and try not to fall off. In practice this requires mastery, and in order to know how to ride a bike the learner has to actually engage in the process, possibly falling off a few times as they do it! This 'knowing how' is often equated with skills, and skill acquisition, and we know that in arts education some skills are general, and some are artform specific, and so the 'knowing how' component of skill is an important one, but do skills exist separately?

In arts education the two types are also combined for a number of artforms and artistic endeavours. Knowing that in order to play an F sharp on a clarinet a certain combination of keys have to pressed, combined with a certain strength of blowing, does not guarantee that the results will be perfect and melodious! To do this, the player needs to know how to play an F sharp, combining the two types of knowing. Likewise a pupil can be aware that pottery involves shaping with the fingers, but until they have actually tried to do it they will not have a real *knowing how* understanding of what is involved. But these are not the only knowledge types we need to be aware of. Specific to music education, Swanwick and Taylor added to the types of knowledge we have been discussing:

- Know how: … to spell a word … to manipulate a musical instrument
- Knowing that: … 2+7=9 … Beethoven wrote nine symphonies
- Knowing him/her/it: … a painting … specific knowledge of a musical work
- Knowing what's what: … what we like …what we value.

(Swanwick and Taylor 1982: 7)

With regard to the third of these, Swanwick expanded upon it somewhat in a later work,

the absolutely central core involved in knowing music can be appropriately called 'knowledge by acquaintance'. … We might call acquaintance knowledge knowing 'this'; knowing *this* person, *this* place, *this* symphony, *this* song.

(Swanwick 1994:17 [original emphasis])

These knowledge types are not only pertinent to music education, they are also relevant to arts education more widely. Indeed, Bertrand Russell writes of 'knowledge by acquaintance' in his study of the problems of philosophy (Russell 1912: 33), where this is acquired by what he refers to as 'sense-data'. Philpott synthesises the types of knowledge, and proposes three types:

- Knowledge about …
- Knowledge how …
- Knowledge of …

(Philpott 2007: 29–30)

This provides one set of ways of thinking about the various knowledge types we shall encounter in cross-curricular teaching and learning. Another way is to separate knowledge from the knower, and ask what might be the characteristics of someone who is knowledgeable in the arts. An example of these being found in the work of Vivian Gadsden, who suggests that this would include:

1. The arts as a way of human knowing—of imagination, aesthetic knowledge, and translation to practical knowledge;
2. The arts as cultural knowledge and as differential cultural knowledge;
3. The arts as traditional (visual, musical, dance, theater, and aesthetics) and emerging genres (e.g., new modalities, media, and technologies); and
4. Interpretation and performance as fundamental concepts.

(Gadsden 2008: 42–3)

This classification is also helpful in considering the general and artform specific types of knowledge that we would want to include.

To take directly one of the knowledge types we have been describing, 'knowing about' and applying it to our discussion so far, we know that there are a variety of knowledge types in the arts, and that we are likely to want to foster these in our programmes. What this might look like in terms of a distinction between knowledge types is, however, not entirely clear. To help with this, the work of Anna Sfard is particularly useful.

Two metaphors for learning

In the appropriately entitled *On Two Metaphors for Learning and the Dangers of Choosing Just One* (Sfard 1998), the two metaphors for learning which Anna Sfard discusses are the *acquisition metaphor*, and the *participation metaphor*. In the acquisition metaphor, as its name suggests, the main focus is on gaining knowledge, which as Sfard observes, 'brings to mind the activity of accumulating material goods' (Sfard 1998: 5). What this means is that knowledge takes on the form of a commodity, and can be owned by an individual.

> Since the time of Piaget and Vygotsky, the growth of knowledge in the process of learning has been analysed in terms of concept development. Concepts are to be understood as basic units of knowledge that can be accumulated, gradually refined, and combined to form ever richer cognitive structures
>
> (ibid.)

The acquisition metaphor, on the other hand, involves moving from acquiring knowledge to taking part in some way, in other words 'the permanence of having gives way to the constant flux of doing' (Sfard 1998: 6). This marks a significant change in the ways we can think about learning and knowledge, and for our purposes of cross-curricular learning, there are ramifications for conceptualising learning in an acquisitive fashion, and participatory learning. In designing a programme of learning involving the arts we will want both metaphors to be invoked. We will want some knowledge to be acquired, but we will also want some knowledge to be participatory. The clarinet pupil we considered above needs both acquired knowledge, the correct fingering for F sharp, and participatory knowledge, to actually play the clarinet in order to play the F sharp. Many types of knowledge in the arts will be like this. Indeed, what we do not want is pupils who can only write essays about playing the clarinet, or using a potter's wheel, we want pupils who can actually do these things. This might seem like an extreme example, bordering on the silly, but we do need to think about the learning-doing split in arts education.

Learning and doing in cross-curricular arts

The discussions we have just been having take us to another of the key areas concerned with cross-curricular learning, that of the difference between *learning* and *doing*. This is an important distinction to make, and is one which needs careful addressing, not just in cross-curricular learning, but in the arts more generally.

There can be tendency for *activity* in the arts to be mistaken for *learning*. This is not to decry activity, and certainly is not intended to downplay the role of active learning. However, it is the case that activity is not a substitute for learning, and that whilst keeping the students busy might be considered by some to be a good thing, it does not mean that they will be concomitantly engaged in learning. Indeed, there was a time in the fairly recent past where books were published for arts subjects which were essentially collections of stimuli for artistic endeavour, within which little by way of learning could be discerned. What could be found in them were plenty of ideas for action and activity. But although the borderline between doing and learning can be a very fine one, it does exist; however, and, maybe especially in the arts, some learning can only be evidenced in doing, and some learning has to be participatory (in Sfard's terms), and involve doing.

This distinction is to be found when artistic endeavour is evidenced in achievement. For example, if a student is learning to play the piano, then the evidence of them having successfully mastered various aspects of piano technique is that they are able to play pieces of music on the piano. This is *evidencing learning through achievement*. It is not the same as repetitive doing. The piano learner will get fed up quickly if they never make progress, and are stuck doing five-finger exercises for weeks on end. For the novice pianist, learning to play pieces of music is what they want to do, and they evidence the results of this learning by being able to perform them. This gives a complex relationship between learning and doing, and shown in Figure 3.3.

What Figure 3.3 shows is that there are links between learning and doing, and that evidencing learning through achievement is another part of the learning system, along with learning by doing. The notion of there being links between learning and doing is a useful one to bear in mind when considering the place of the arts as an element in cross-curricular learning, especially in the ways in which the arts are situated in learning projects.

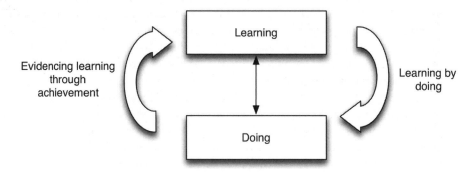

Figure 3.3 Learning and doing.

Linking learning with knowledge

Sfard's view of knowledge, and our discussions on learning and doing, challenge the notion of knowledge as a unitary construct. For example, Scheffler (1999) posits three philosophies of knowledge, the rationalist, the empiricist, and the pragmatic. In the rationalist view of knowledge, the field of mathematics is held to be the prime model. Mathematical knowledge is not dependent on personal experience, nor does it need experimentation. It is a pure form of knowledge, capable of demonstration, and also capable of falsification. In contrast to this, in the empiricist view, natural science is the model. Investigation reveal truths about the world, logic is required to distinguish what is truth, and, according to this view,

> the ideal education ... trains the student not only in proper logical habits but in traits requisite for learning from experience – accurate observation, reasonable generalization, willingness to revise or relinquish purported laws which fail to anticipate the actual course of events
>
> (Scheffler 1999: 3)

Finally, in the pragmatic view, it is experiment that matters, and the individual needs to 'go beyond reasonable generalizations of observed phenomenal patterns in our past experience' (Scheffler 1999: 4). Experimentation involves actively engaging with, and changing aspects of, our environment. It involves learning from experience. What these philosophies have in common is that they are all considered as being located in the mind of a single individual. Knowledge is 'owned' by a person. 'A widely held view of knowledge is that it is stuff that is made and kept in your head; that is, knowledge is a thing of the mind' (Kalantzis and Cope 2008: 159). This view of knowledge, as situated solely in the mind of a single individual is being increasingly challenged in contemporary cognitive psychology. Our discussions of learning by participation are but one form of this. Viewing knowledge in the arts as a social activity can have important ramifications for the ways in which learning is conceptualised, and it is to that which we now turn our attention.

Thinking about learning

Reflective task

What happens when you want to know something? What do you do?

The answer to this question probably takes one of two forms:

1. You ask someone.

2. You look it up, probably on the Internet.

If the question is of a personal nature, like 'when is Uncle so-and-so's birthday?', you will ask a family member. If it is almost anything else you will either look it up in a book, or, in today's wired age, more probably look on the Internet. So, whose is the knowledge on the Internet? Do you need to know everything on it? Could you? Where is the knowledge contained by the Internet? Whose knowledge is it? If it is on the Internet and you have looked it up can you be said to have learned it? What does it mean to have learned anything?

These are all difficult questions. They bring to the fore the discussions we had earlier concerning knowledge, that of learning as a solitary accomplishment, or one which is undertaken in social situations. To investigate this we need to think about learning and, in particular, theoretical accounts of learning, and what we can take from them concerning the ways in which our students are learning things in the arts.

A comprehensive review of learning theories is beyond the scope of this book, and we need to limit our views to a manageable size. This is compounded by the fact that as Strauss observes, 'notions of learning and development are neither fixed nor agreed upon' (Strauss 2000: 31). Following Mary James (2006) it seems logical to classify learning theories under three headings:

- Behaviourist
- Cognitive and constructivist
- Socio-cultural, situated, and activity theories

(James 2006: 54–6)

What we are particularly interested in is what these families of theories have to tell us about learning with relation to the arts, and what we can take from them when we think about devising more explicit cross-curricular programmes of learning.

Behaviourism and learning in the arts

Behaviourists believe that learning is a set of responses to stimuli. This theoretical approach is exemplified in the famous experiment of Pavlov, where he found that dogs would salivate when presented with food, and that making a sounds at the same time as food was presented would ultimately lead to the dogs salivating at the sound alone. The process of presenting food and sound is called *conditioning*, and once the dogs associates the sound with the food, this is a *conditioned response*. What behaviourists believe this means is that learning, in animals or humans, is conditioned by stimuli. The key aspects of behaviourism, is this stimulus-response (S-R) cycle. Responses can be *reinforced* by punishment (some of the behavioural experiments of B.F. Skinner involved giving animals small electric shocks if they did things they were not supposed to!), or by positive reinforcement involving pleasure or a reward (for animals this would often be food). One of the problems with this view is that:

> Any introspection into the processes of learning was seen by behaviorists as neither reliable nor relevant to the understanding of behavioral processes
>
> (Gruhn and Rauscher 2006: 41)

One of the implications of this view is that reducing intelligence to a single characteristic, measurable by the IQ (intelligence quotient) test is deeply problematic. Indeed, some commentators have argued that:

For all their experiments and 'scientific' investigations, much of the behaviourist psychology is conceptually flawed. ... The basic concepts they used (such as the distinction between knowledge and intelligence) were fundamentally flawed

(Kalantzis and Cope 2008: 147)

This causes problems for the arts, with some problematic aspects of perception reduced to what Arthur Efland refers to as 'mere ephemera' (Efland 2002: 18). Indeed, Efland goes on to observe that:

Behaviorism never adequately explained the emergence of higher-order thinking abilities through the formation of such [S-R] connections, nor did it explain the specific factors in stimuli that activate the arousal of feelings and emotions given play by works of art.

(Efland 2002: 48)

Although there are learned behaviours in the arts, few nowadays would assert, as classical behaviourists did, that these take place without reference to higher mental functioning; in other words it is acknowledged that some form of cognitive functioning is involved. Having said this, many aspects of schools can still be seen to operate on behaviourist principles, with notions of punishment and reward being clearly visible.

Cognitive and constructivist learning and the arts

Cognitive learning theories involve the brain, and involve mental processes such as perception, memory and information processing. Constructivist views of learning can be thought of as arising from cognitive viewpoints, and involve seeing the learners as being actively involved in *constructing* their own meanings. An early exponent of constructivism was Piaget, who considered that children pass through a series of stages as maturation occurs, and that as they develop they become able to learn things of increasing complexity. Another key figure, who straddles cognitive and constructivist approaches, is Jerome Bruner. Bruner (1966) observed that as maturation occurs, children need to develop key intellectual skills in order to be able to deal with the information that is presented to them. He identified three stages in this:

Enactive: In this stage the learner is directly involved in activity
Iconic: Here the knowledge in question can be represented by a mental image
Symbolic: More abstract, based in language, where descriptions using words can also be used for reflection

As cognitive and constructivist perspectives acknowledge the role of mind, as a function of brain, there are many possible applications of this when considering teaching and learning in the arts. Indeed, one of the strengths of arts education can be seen to be in taking the symbolic perspective beyond words, and into artform-specific higher-order thinking.

Socio-cultural theories

Human learning takes place in a social context. We learn language from those around us, and we learn how to do things from others. Importantly, in human beings, this learning leads to *understanding*, and it is this that marks us out as being different from other animals. Lev Vygotsky was a Russian psychologist working in the early part of the twentieth century, but whose work did not become known in the West until long after his death, who believed that everything we learn begins as a social experience, then moves to becoming personalised within an individual later:

> Every function in the child's cultural development appears twice: first, on the social level, and later, on the individual level; first, between people ('interpsychological') and then inside the child ('intrapsychological'). This applies equally to voluntary attention, to logical memory, and to the formation of concepts. All the higher functions originate as actual relationships between individuals.
>
> (Vygotsky 1978: 57)

What this means is that individuals learn from those around them, therefore from society, and from the culture, hence the 'socio-cultural' labelling of these theories.

Vygotsky is possibly best known for his description of the *zone of proximal development*, (ZPD). The ZPD is described as the area which lies between what children are able to accomplish by themselves at present, and what they will be able to do with some assistance in the future. What he said was: 'what the child is able to do in collaboration today he [sic] will be able to do independently tomorrow' (Vygotsky 1987: 211). This has serious ramifications for us in thinking about cross-curricular learning in the arts, as the ZPD means that students working collaboratively will, in effect, be working in their respective zones of proximal development, and that this is an integral part of what is going on. This means that, 'group work is not an optional extra' (James 2006: 57). It is, however, important to note that 'the zone of proximal development is not simply a way to refer to development through assistance by a more competent other' (Chaiklin, 2003: 57), but that it can be used to account for the differences which can be made to learning which in turn lead to development.

Situated and activity theories

The socio-cultural viewpoint also includes the important linked areas of situated learning, distributed cognition and activity theory. Situated learning involves the learner being involved in societal situations where doing, and therefore learning, is shared between members of the group. What is important here is the idea of there being a *community of practice* (Lave and Wenger 1991). What Lave and Wenger describe is the shift from novice towards expert involvement in the activity, and that:

> learners inevitably participate in communities of practitioners and that the mastery of knowledge and skill requires newcomers to move toward full participation in the sociocultural practices of a community
>
> (Lave and Wenger 1991: 29)

For our purposes this has clear links to cross-curricular learning and teaching involving the arts. We have already seen how important group work is in developing pupil learning; here the notion of situated learning means that there is learning done whilst engaged in the social situation of group process. This has ramifications not only for the group, but also for the individuals within it. Indeed, another aspect of socio-cultural learning is the notion of *distributed cognition* (Salomon 1993), where cognitive process are, literally, *shared between* members of a group. This can be seen in cross-curricular arts projects where collaborative creativity projects are involved, where the cognitive distribution of creativity is distributed amongst the members of the group, and the creative processes are jointly owned by the members of that group. Real-life examples are to be found, amongst others, in improvisatory theatre companies and jazz quartets (Sawyer 2003).

Closely allied with both situated learning and distributed cognition is activity theory. Activity theory takes as its unit of analysis 'the concept of object-oriented, collective, and culturally mediated human activity' (Engeström *et al.* 1999) It also

> insists upon [,] a pedagogic imagination that reflects on the processes of teaching and learning as much more than face-to-face interaction or the simple transmission of prescribed knowledge and skill.
>
> (Daniels 2004)

Activity theory is helpful in illuminating the ways in which complex activity systems operate, and many classroom cross-curricular teaching and learning programmes can usefully be considered using it.

But how is this view of socio-cultural learning represented in schools? Lucas and Claxton observe that, 'the world has never been a more networked place, yet for the most part schools remain stubbornly focused on individuals' (Lucas and Claxton 2010: 111). It is here that cross-curricular teaching and learning arts programmes come into play. We are not concerned solely with the development of individualised, isolationist learning. Teachers will want to personalise the learning that they offer, but this does not mean they have break it up into separate components, and then parcel it out amongst the students, but instead that thought is given to the sorts of things that will be relevant to specific learner cohorts, and plan and enact accordingly.

Reflective task

Think about some aspects of educational provision, either in single subjects, or in cross-curricular teaching and learning. What aspects:

Involve group work?

Require collaboration?

Require inter-personal skills?

Facilitate learners working in the ZPD?

Allow learners to construct meaning?

Enable learning through doing?

Pupil knowledge and teacher knowledge

So far we have been considering the forms and types of knowledge which we will want the pupils to be developing. But what of the teacher? What does the teacher need to know which is separate from the knowledge of the pupils?

Reflective task

What do you need to know before you begin to teach a topic?

Is it good enough, like the hairdresser in the story earlier this chapter observed, to be simply two pages ahead in the textbook? Is there a textbook in your subject? Few arts disciplines have anything as methodical as sequenced learning materials unless it has been prepared by the staff in the school, do you?

So, what more than the pupils do you know, or need to know?

One of the key answers to this reflective task is that you not only need to know subject content, but you also need to know how to teach it. This is where atheoretical approaches to teaching and learning are found wanting. In atheoretical approaches it is assumed that good subject knowledge is sufficient, and that teaching is simply telling. This nineteenth century view is no longer good enough. Teachers need specialist subject knowledge, certainly, but they also need to know about learning, and how to teach. Shulman writes of the different types of knowledge needed by teachers, which he refers to as *pedagogic content knowledge* (PCK). Pedagogic content knowledge includes:

> the most useful forms of representation of those ideas, the most powerful analogies, illustrations, examples, explanations, and demonstrations – in a word, the ways of representing and formulating the subject that make it comprehensible to others.
>
> (Shulman 1986: 9)

This is what you will be doing as a teacher. You will be endeavouring to make things 'comprehensible to others'. Another aspect of PCK which Shulman described is that of *curricular knowledge*, of which he observed that

> I would expect a professional teacher to be familiar with the curriculum materials under study by his or her students in other subjects they are studying at the same time
>
> (Shulman 1986: 10)

Shulman also notes that this is unlikely! But it is a useful link back to our discussions in Chapter 1 concerning curriculum mapping, and, in the case of multi-staff cross-curricular teaching and learning projects, will be absolutely key in ensuring smooth transition between learners, teachers and areas of content, and is likely to become more important as cross-curricular work becomes more embedded.

Having considered learning, knowledge, and the types of activity that can take place in cross-curricular teaching and learning programmes in the arts, let us now turn to an investigation of another case study, this time of a project where there was a distinctive pedagogy.

Case Study: 'The Mantle of the Expert'

At Queensbridge school in Birmingham, a number of cross-curricular learning projects have been developed for use in Year 7 (Fautley *et al.* in press). These involve students working in imagined contexts within which learning takes place. The pedagogy for this is based on the work of Dorothy Heathcote, who devised the notion of the 'Mantle of the Expert':

> The Mantle of the Expert is a dramatic-inquiry based approach to teaching and learning invented and developed by Professor Dorothy Heathcote at the University of Newcastle upon Tyne in the 1980's. The big idea is that the class do all their curriculum work as if they are an imagined group of experts. They might be scientists in a laboratory or archaeologists excavating a tomb, or a rescue team at the scene of a disaster. They might be running a removal company, or a factory, or a shop, or a space station or a French resistance group. Because they behave 'as if they are experts', the children are working from a specific point of view as they explore their learning and this brings special responsibilities, language needs and social behaviours.
>
> (MoE website n.d.)

This is a distinctive pedagogy originating in drama, which requires the teacher to consider a number of areas simultaneously:

- Activity is social and collaborative – students work together negotiating meaning while sharing and deepening their understanding.
- It fuses our capacity to be emotionally affected by a situation with our ability to reason about it – it works within a fiction where there is always something at stake for the people in the story.
- It requires inquiry into values – implications and consequences of action are scrutinised from inside a dilemma and from differing standpoints.
- It exploits the human capacity for liminality – so that we can tolerate ambiguity as we're on the threshold of new understandings that bring our own knowledge and experience into focus.
- It uses the critical dramatic elements of tension and constraint.
- It operates in the urgency of 'now' time.

(Gee in press)

Gavin Bolton, who worked with Heathcote for many years, noted that:

> the essential nature of her work is bound up with her assumption that dramatic action, by its nature, is subordinated to meaning, Such a notion goes back to 1933 when Vygotsky first made the following comment about child make-believe play. He writes: 'In play a child deals with things as having meaning'. He suggests that whereas in 'real life' action is prioritised over meaning, the opposite occurs in make-believe. It seems to me that everything Dorothy Heathcote said about her work in those early attempts at explanation stemmed from this assumption ... that dramatic action was to do with attending to meaning, or rather meanings, to be negotiated with her class and leading to action
>
> (Bolton 1998: 76)

One of the fictions which the Year 7 students worked in was that of a witness protection unit (WPU). Here the learners were working at finding out what happens in a WPU, and then working through fictive situations as they evolved. In doing this, the students needed to investigate the communities where the suspects and witnesses lived. They needed to know about the community so that later, as WPU members, they could evaluate potential threats that might come from within it. This was a dialogic approach which added both breadth and depth to the fictional world within which the WPU episode took place. As a teacher involved observed:

> They also played the gang members because we started to look at the gang and what it's like to be part of the gang. They played members of their families because we're looking at migration of people into Birmingham and a look at the generation gap between the gang members and their parents and grandparents. So they're having to look at ritual, religion and behaviour and manners and etiquette and all that kind of stuff ... as WPU we're doing files on individual gang members ... (using) drama to uncover key moments.
>
> (Fautley et al. 2008: 46)

This led to a wide range of activities and curricular coverage. For example, here is how aspects of the geography curriculum had been absorbed into the process, so that the knowledge, skills, and understandings involved all had coherence for the students:

> They have done Google earth and they went on the computer and they each had a satellite image, which is part of what they have to do with Geography, and then they had to locate the gang territory ... find areas of ambush ... look at land usage. It's all necessary for the fiction to continue. And then they would come and cross reference with that map and do grid

references and the next stage is, they can have groups, one of them is undercover and briefed outside and we found a new piece of evidence and they have to very quickly work out directions using that map in order for the undercover officer to get to Kelly's house before anything happens. So, again, there is a tension in that. So they're having to manipulate all the knowledge base in order to complete their jobs as WPU … we have to look at this in order to keep Kelly and her family safe … there is a need to know. The urgency is – she's in danger, right, so – who is on Taylor Road? Right – who's got the grid reference quick – so … you are all people in on it together rather than we (the teachers) are the people who know.

(Fautley *et al*. 2008: 43)

This was with Year 7 students, and deals with subject matter which often would be considered to be the province of older students. What working within the convention of the Mantle of the Expert did was to allow teachers and students to delimit the areas which were appropriate to the pupils, whilst still stretching them:

This allowed teachers and children to interrogate, safely, subject matter which would ordinarily only be dealt with by older students. This is because, using drama, the problems, the dilemmas, the students dealt with were as difficult as they agreed them to be. They were protected into experience, always aware that they were creating a fictional world but one which was truthful.

(Fautley *et al*. 2008: 43)

One of the teachers involved spoke about student engagement with this process, where the students were co-constructors of their own learning:

they love being in role as WPU (Witness Protection Unit) they love having the responsibility, they love seeing that they can influence the course of events. They love seeing that they have ownership of materials … whatever they do in one lesson is then fed into the next lesson. They love the freedom but also the discipline of it because, of course, it is very disciplined.

(Fautley *et al*. 2008: 40)

To do this required a degree of flexibility from the teachers, and at times involved them responding to the learners, as this teacher observed:

Every lesson doesn't have to be totally prescriptive. We don't say, right, we're going to do this in this lesson, this is all we're going to do. You know if the pupils think of something that wants to take them off (my) track then we're quite confident and happy to do that.

(Fautley *et al*. 2008: 44)

By working in this way the learners were acting with constructivist and socio-cultural approaches to learning. Doing this is more likely to lead to deep learning, and, especially, to that key educational goal, understanding,

> Understanding consists in grasping the place of an idea or fact in some more general structure of knowledge ... Acquired knowledge is most useful to a learner, moreover, when it is 'discovered' through the learner's own cognitive efforts, for it is then related to and used in reference to what one has known before. Such acts of discovery are enormously facilitated by the structure of knowledge itself, for however complicated any domain of knowledge may be, it can be represented in ways that make it accessible through less complex elaborated processes. It was this conclusion that led me to propose that any subject could be taught to any child at any age in some form that was honest.
>
> (Bruner 1996: xi–xii)

Teaching and learning involving the Mantle of the Expert approach in this fashion does, of course, require a different form of pedagogic content knowledge to operationalise the learning encounter than might normally be expected. However, the benefits for both teachers and pupils were felt by those involved to be significant.

For this case study of a real cross-curricular teaching and learning programme in a school, it is clear that a number of difficult topics are addressed during the course of it. This raises the question of what sorts of knowledge are valued, and by whom. So to return to our consideration of the nature of knowledge, it is this question that we now address.

Knowledge and power

In this part of our discussion concerning knowledge we turn our attention to addressing issues concerning the stratification of knowledge into a hierarchy, in other words the reasons some sorts of knowledge tend to be seen as being more valuable than others. In schools this can be seen within subjects, as well as between them. Knowing how to calculate the odds of a horse winning according to bookkeepers' odds may be a useful skill for some, but is not likely to figure highly in many school maths syllabi! In a similar fashion, knowing about the origins and powers of Superman is not likely to be covered in English literature courses. Neither of these are seen as items of knowledge which are particularly valued by the educational system. Between subjects the curricular 'heavyweights' of maths, English, and science are accorded more time and resources than subjects which are seen as peripheral. All of these issues are to do with the valorisation of knowledge, and of the placing of more importance on some forms of knowledge compared with others. As Young asks: 'the power of some to define what is "valued" knowledge leads to the question of accounting for how knowledge is stratified, and by what criteria' (Young 1999: 99). Knowledge does not just exist, it exists as result of a power struggle, 'history is written by the victors', as Winston Churchill is alleged to have said. What this means is that there is power to be had in owning certain types of knowledge, and that in some quarters having knowledge is itself an act of power. The notion of knowledge as power was discussed by Foucault:

> we should abandon a whole tradition that allows us to imagine that knowledge can exist only where the power relations are suspended and that knowledge can develop only outside its injunctions, its demands and its interests ... We should admit rather that power produced knowledge ... that power and knowledge directly imply one another; that there is no power relation without the correlative constitution of a field of knowledge
>
> (Foucault 1979: 27)

This is a problematic viewpoint. If we abandon the tradition of power in knowledge in educational terms, with what do we replace it? The relationship between power and knowledge is complex and, it could be argued, played out in arenas distant from the school and classroom. Or is it? The power allotted to various bodies of knowledge in the school curriculum is the most obvious manifestation of this in the terms we are considering:

> those areas of knowledge perceived to be more powerful are able to augment their power through greater access to curriculum time and institutional space. Pre-eminent among these are mathematics, science and information technology, although (in English speaking countries) English can command time (but not so easily space)
>
> (Paechter 2000: 30)

For cross-curricular learning this can result in curricular power struggles in the staffroom when cross-curricular learning ideas are mooted. This is because in current formulations the identity of a teacher in the secondary school is often bound up very strongly within an individual subject specialism. We looked at teacher identities in Chapter 1, here we are revisiting this issue.

Many teachers have constructed their identities from within the boundaries of their subject

---

Reflective task

Here are some possible stereotypes, what do you think of when you hear the phrase:

The male PE teacher

The geography teacher

The art teacher

The woodwork teacher

For some teachers, attempts to break down boundaries between subjects are seen as troublesome, and to be resisted; in Bernstein's terms, this is regarded as 'pollution' of the purity of the single subject specialism:

> A sense of the sacred, the 'otherness' of educational knowledge, I submit does not arise so much out of an ethic of knowledge for its own sake, but is more a function of socialization into subject loyalty: for it is the subject which becomes the linchpin of the identity. Any attempt to weaken or change classification strength may be felt as a threat to one's identity and may be experienced as a pollution endangering the sacred.
>
> (Bernstein 1971:56)

This is a point that will need to be borne in mind, maybe in the reflective task concerning stereotyping above you could feel the draw of 'socialization into subject loyalty', which the teachers might feel. Maybe you feel this yourself too? However, what can happen is that this can affect how cross-curricular projects can potentially be maximised for their learning potential. What this means is that for some teachers there can be an initial reluctance to relinquish what they perceive to be control of the curriculum. The hegemonic view that Carrie Paechter described above is an example of how this might be reified in staffroom politics. But this potentially pessimistic view needs to be tempered with the excitement that new ways of learning can engender amongst pupils, and this carries its own momentum. Maybe the needs of the pupils should outweigh the identity issues of the staff? This is a question which requires some hard thinking!

SEAL and PLTS

We have covered a great deal of ground in our thinking about planning derived from Figure 1.1. The question that follows that of thinking about which aspects of the arts will be learned involves considering which aspects of social and emotional aspects of learning (SEAL) will be covered, and which aspects of personal learning and thinking skills (PLTS). We looked at PLTS in Chapter 1, and the point to add from this current chapter is that we have also introduced thinking as a social activity into the mix. This leads us to SEAL, and here it should be clear that, in our recognition of the social component involved in the socio-cultural elements of cross-curricular learning, we have identified this as being fundamental to the enterprise. Social aspects of learning are fundamental to the ways in which cross-curricular teaching and learning in the arts projects are often conceived. We have seen how Lave and Wenger's notion of *communities of practice* is important in arts learning. Allied to this Vygotsky's description of the ZPD means that we will expect our pupils to be working cooperatively, and social learning, learning in groups, will be a normal methodology.

Emotional aspects of learning will often be an integral component of learning in the arts, indeed it is this area which can give arts-based learning significant leverage in educational circles. To this end the important aspect from a planning perspective is to consider ways in which learners can emotionally identify with the work being undertaken; in the case study above, for example, the way the pupils were working in the witness protection unit project.

Artform-specific concepts and skills

This takes us to the next of the important questions, that of which artform-specific concepts and skills will be learned.

We have been looking at generalised aspects of cross-curricular learning, but there will be aspects of learning which teachers of the arts will want addressed with regard to their own subject areas. This area was looked at initially in Chapter 2. The questions for us now include: what are skills, what are they in the context of a single artform, and how should they be dealt with in cross-curricular teaching ?

In the section *knowledge and power* above, we considered the values associated with certain types of knowledge. Not dissimilar notions of valorisation can be seen with regard to skills. For example, here is Lucy Green writing about singing soul music, and how the philosopher Roger Scruton downgrades this skill:

> The almost complete absence of any formal educational mechanisms for singing soul … gives the appearance that excellence in this feat requires no education, and must be very easy to achieve. Scruton … exemplifies this dilemma: 'The assumption has been that we teach classical music because it requires disciplined study. Expertise in pop, on the other hand, can be acquired by osmosis' (1996). Typically, he has no grounds for this latter claim.

(Green 2000: 99)

Here Scruton is valuing classical music, and saying that expertise in popular music is simple, and is easily acquired by being exposed to it.

Reflective task

Think of an artform specific skill, possibly from your own subject area. Are there skills which historically might not be valued in educational settings?

There are many areas of human and artistic endeavour which school students will work at acquiring. Here are some:

Skateboarding	Rapping
Graffitti and Tagging	Impressions
Street dancing	Stand-up comedy
Blogging	Website design
Text messaging	Fashion

Where do these figure in the school curriculum, or are they excluded, and is this exclusion justified?

This leads to the question as to what skills are valued in schools. Are some skills learned simply because teachers feel they should be, rather than serving any real-life or contemporary purpose?

Reflective story

I spent many hours at school in maths lessons learning to use a slide-rule. Many of you may not even know what a slide-rule is nowadays! Is there an equivalent skill in your subject that might be outdated in the future? Does it matter?

We are equipping our learners to deal with a future which we do not really know about yet.[1] As the then DfEE observed back in 1997:

> Children cannot be effective in tomorrow's world if they are trained in yesterday's skills
> (DfEE 1997: foreword)

Are the skills we want our students to have fit for purpose? There is some anecdotal evidence that changes in the UK National Curriculum have not been accompanied by changes in curricula at the level of the individual school. We know that teachers can find change difficult, How many art and design teachers would agree with this statement, for example?

> we are still delivering art curricula in our schools predicated largely upon procedures and practices which reach back to the nineteenth century – procedures and practices which cling to a comfortable and uncontentious view of art and its purposes.
> (Hughes 2002: 41)

Art and design in the twenty-first century involves an array of image-making and editing software that come freely pre-installed on many of the computers that the learners will have access to at home. The same is true of music-making and editing programmes. And instant action and game-based programmes allow virtual actors and avatars to play roles in dramatic situations which could never be realised by lone pupils. This calls for a reappraisal of what skills are required, and is a theme we return to in our consideration of ICT in Chapter 5.

What this means is that the days of teaching and learning in the arts involving an accretion of disparate skills in a semi-atomistic fashion is no longer sufficient. Of course skills are still needed, and expertise in the arts is associated with a developed skill base. But operationalising skill acquisition without a corresponding development in teaching for understanding is to denigrate the importance of the arts. And so it is to a discussion of the notion of 'understanding' that we now turn.

The role of understanding

'Understanding' is a deceptively simple word, but what does it entail? We discussed some of the work of the Project Zero team at Harvard in earlier chapters. They have also looked into this question, as one of the members, David Perkins, explains:

At the heart of teaching for understanding lies a very basic question: What is understanding? Ponder this query for a moment and you will realize that good answers are not obvious. To draw a comparison, we all have a reasonable conception of what knowing is. When a student knows something, the student can bring it forth upon call--tell us the knowledge or demonstrate the skill. But understanding something is a more subtle matter. A student might be able to regurgitate reams of facts and demonstrate routine skills with very little understanding. Somehow, understanding goes beyond knowing.

He continues:

My colleagues and I at the Harvard Graduate School of Education have analyzed the meaning of understanding as a concept. We have examined views of understanding in contemporary research and looked to the practices of teachers with a knack for teaching for understanding. We have formulated a conception of understanding consonant with these several sources. We call it a "performance perspective" on understanding. This perspective reflects the general spirit of "constructivism" prominent in contemporary theories of learning … and offers a specific view of what learning for understanding involves. This perspective helps to clarify what understanding is and how to teach for understanding by making explicit what has been implicit and making general what has been phrased in more restricted ways … In brief, this performance perspective says that understanding a topic of study is a matter of being able to perform in a variety of thought-demanding ways with the topic, for instance to: explain, muster evidence, find examples, generalize, apply concepts, analogize, represent in a new way, and so on.

(Perkins 1993)

Understanding, from this perspective, is focused on the performance of the learner. This is not performance from a performing arts perspective (although it could be!), but is to do with the ways in which the learner is able to engage with the subject matter, and demonstrate their thinking, not just *by* application, but *in* application. 'Teaching for understanding' is a commonly heard mantra of contemporary education, but conceptualised like this it is more than simply knowing a lot about a subject, it is being able to operate *within* the subject. In Lave and Wenger's terms it involves operating from within a community of practice. Teaching for understanding, therefore, is a desideratum of cross-curricular learning. In the witness protection unit scheme detailed above, there is clear evidence that the pupils were developing their understandings by working from an insider perspective on the tasks involved.

But how can we develop understanding in the arts? Consider this statement from Ofsted:

The National Curriculum for art and design deliberately does not define precisely what is to be covered. This is so that individual schools can develop a curriculum that meets the needs and interests of their pupils. The programmes of study are intended to provide a broad definition of expectations in each key stage. Because of the lack of detail, the teachers interviewed during the survey had struggled, often with minimal professional development, to design a curriculum that enabled pupils to build a progression of skills, knowledge and understanding across a broad range of art, craft and design from different times and cultures. It is not surprising that, because of a lack of alternatives, many primary teachers had resorted to published schemes of work and secondary teachers to adapting schemes of work that existed before the National Curriculum.

(Ofsted 2009a: 21)

Notice the phrase 'struggled … to design a curriculum that enabled pupils to build a progression of skills, knowledge and understanding'. This is precisely the point, understanding needs to be built in, and planned for in the way it will be dealt with in schemes of work.

In drama, Baldwin and Fleming (2003: 40) remind us that we need to think about understanding in terms of cognitive and affective domains. This is important, and it is worth considering what these terminologies entail. There is little doubt that using the Mantle of the Expert in the WPU scheme facilitated emotional engagement by the learners in the topic in question, this being an aspect of affective understanding. But what are cognitive and affective understandings?

The most well known work in this area is that of Benjamin Bloom and his associates, who developed the well-known Bloom's taxonomy of educational objectives for the cognitive domain back in 1956 (Bloom 1956). Less well known is the taxonomy of educational objectives for the affective domain which appeared some years later (Bloom *et al.* 1964). Bloom and his colleagues found this much harder to investigate and write about, and say so in the introduction, along with the observation that they were less happy with the results:

As is indicated in the text, we found the affective domain much more difficult to structure, and we are much less satisfied with the result. Our hope is, however, that it will represent enough of an advance in the field to call attention to the problems of affective-domain terminology.

(Bloom *et al.* 1964: vii)

The affective domain taxonomy has received comparatively little attention, but it does have some merits in delineating aspects of affective response that can be thought about. The cognitive taxonomy, on the other hand, has received a great deal of attention, and figures highly in a number of governmental publications. What is less well known in the UK, however, is the recent work of the American educational researcher Robert Marzano, who has devised a new taxonomy of educational objectives, which are highly appropriate for our thinking in cross-curricular teaching and learning in the arts. Marzano's taxonomy is based on three domains of knowledge and six levels of processing. The first four levels of processing, involving the cognitive system are:

- Retrieval
- Comprehension
- Analysis
- Knowledge utilization

(Marzano and Kendall 2007: 13)

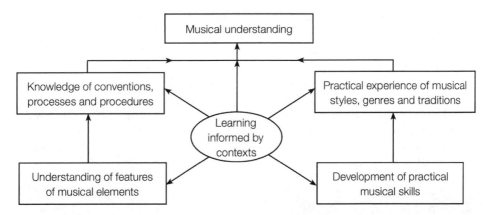

Figure 3.4 Secondary Strategy model of musical understanding (source: DfES 2006: 6).

This shows that the lower level skills of retrieval and comprehension precede the higher level skills of analysis and knowledge utilisation.

The case for including affective and cognitive domains when thinking about drama takes us on to the role of understanding in music, where in the Secondary Strategy support materials the role of understanding was placed at the pinnacle, as Figure 3.4 shows.

The effect of the thinking evidenced in Figure 3.4 is to treat skills, knowledge and concepts as leading towards the goal of musical understanding. Whilst this is clearly a subject-specific model, nonetheless having understanding as a goal is an important notion to bear in mind, and the flowchart shown in Figure 3.4 could be redrawn for cross-curricular learning projects in and across the arts as they are being planned.

Practical task

Can you redraw Figure 3.4 for:

a) Your own subject?

b) A cross-curricular teaching and learning programme?

What issues are there? What aspects of skills leading towards understanding do you need to consider?

Concluding remarks

This chapter has looked in some detail at a number of aspects of pedagogy and practice in cross-curricular teaching and learning. From this two key messages can be drawn:

- Planning is vital
- Teachers need to be responsive to different ways of working

Both of these messages are reiterated a number of times throughout this book, and its companions in the series. Indeed, as we saw in Chapter 1, one of the overarching themes of this series of books is that there can be 'no curriculum development without teacher development' (Stenhouse 1980: 85). The responses of the teachers to the witness protection unit schemes are key examples of this. Here teachers act as facilitators of learning, and provide a steer when required. This is a long way from the didactic 'chalk and talk' role where learners are treated as empty vessels.

One of the key aspects missing from this chapter, which received its own box in Figure 3.1 has been that of assessment. This is because assessment is such a key issue that it warrants a later chapter of its own. However, before we turn to matters of assessment, we need to consider the areas of language, and of the role of ICT. And so it is to those which we turn next.

Summary

This has been a wide-ranging chapter! We have looked at a number of aspects of pedagogy, from a consideration of what is involved in pedagogy, to ways in which various pedagogies can be enacted using case study exemplar materials. We have again emphasised the key role of planning for teaching and learning. Socio-cultural views of learning have been seen to be important, and we have spent some time investigating the cooperative nature of much learning involving the arts, including Vygotsky's key notion of the Zone of Proximal Development. Knowledge, its typologies, and the ways it can be acquired and participated in have also been central to our inquiries in this chapter, and we have thought about differences between learning and doing. Shulman's idea of pedagogic content knowledge has proved useful in thinking about teacher pedagogies, and we have thought about how some types of knowledge are valued more highly than others. Finally, we reflected on how a key goal of education should be that of understanding, and the role of skill development was to lead towards this.

Meeting the Standards

This chapter will help you meet the following Q standards for ITT:
Q6, Q7a, Q10, Q14, Q15, Q18, Q22, Q25b and c, Q29

Professional Standards for Teachers

This chapter will help you meet the following core standards:
C6, C7, C10, C15, C18, C26, C29b,c and e, C39, C40

Notes

1. For some interesting insights into this, look on the Internet for the presentation *Shift Happens* in various forms.

The language of cross-curricular teaching and learning in the arts

Key objectives

By the end of this chapter, you will be able to:

■ See how new approaches to cross-curricular teaching and learning in the arts helps teachers and pupils develop new types of expressive, artistic languages.

■ Consider how language and communication within the arts is distinctive from other areas of the curriculum.

■ Explore how metaphors can help make connections across arts practices and apply this to your own work.

Preamble

During the first half of this book, we have established a broad framework for the principles of cross-curricular teaching and learning in the arts and examined how this outworks through the construction of a skilful pedagogy and classroom practice. This chapter, and the following two, will take a more detailed look at a number of specific aspects of teaching and learning that can be developed through a cross-curricular approach. These chapters will draw on ideas discussed in the overarching, generic publication (Savage 2011) and apply them to teaching and learning within the arts. This chapter explores the 'language' of cross-curricularity within the arts; Chapter 5 considers the use of information and communication technologies (ICT) as tools that empower cross-curricular approaches within the arts curriculum; and Chapter 6 moves on to consider assessment and how a more cross-curricular artistic approach can usefully inform our work as arts educators. In contrast with the previous chapters, these three chapters can be considered as more detailed, explorative approaches to key, common elements of all arts teachers' pedagogy. As such, we hope that they provide a broader rationale for further studies on the development of cross-curricular teaching and learning within the arts.

Introduction

Language is an integral element within all teaching and learning processes. In various forms, it underpins our communication with students and is a vital element for effective teaching and learning. For this reason, the majority of students undertaking initial teacher education are asked to analyse issues such as developing good explanations, effective questioning strategies, developing the pupil voice and similar issues within their studies. This chapter is not going to re-rehearse these well-established arguments. There are plenty of sources of support for that already.

But some readers may be surprised by the inclusion of this chapter at all! After all, are not issues of language, and its close cousin literacy, the preserve of teachers elsewhere in the school – particular our English colleagues? Not so. Language and literacy are the preserve of all teachers. As one colleague said to me in my first year of teaching, 'We are all teachers of language, my boy!' As teachers of the arts, we have an advantage here. David Stevens, in his companion title within this series for English teachers, writes that 'throughout my own professional experience I have always considered English to be, fundamentally, an arts-based subject, and I feel this all the more strongly in the context of the interdisciplinary turn we are commending here' (Stevens 2011: 100).He goes on to quote from Abbs (1982) who, from the outset of his book, announces that:

> My main intention will be to argue for a concept of English as a literary expressive discipline, a discipline whose deepest affinities lie … with the arts or what I prefer to call, at least in the context of the curriculum, the expressive disciplines. One of the most important claims I will make is that English should now form strong philosophical, practical and political alliances with the undervalued disciplines of art, dance, drama, music and film.
>
> (Abbs 1982: 7)

Within the book Abbs argued that the alliances he recommended would be mutually beneficial for teachers and students within English and the arts in a number of ways; each would enliven the other in philosophical and practical ways and, perhaps importantly in the current educational climate although we would not want to think this as practitioners, the linking of English to the arts gives the arts enhanced credibility within the curriculum framework in the eyes of policy makers.

Perhaps you are wondering whether Stevens (2011) and Abbs (1982) are overstating their case a little? Stevens' work helps us here by giving some well-worked examples of how these broad statements about English and its link to the arts subjects develop on a subject by subject basis. For music, he considers what might be natural processes that underpin language development and compares these to how early, even pre-natal, musical experiences shape our consciousness. He quotes Pinker, who posits that:

> Language is not a cultural artefact that we learn the way we learn to tell time or how the federal government works. Instead it is a distinct piece of the biological makeup of our brains. Language is a complex, specialised skill, which develops in the child spontaneously, without conscious effort or formal instruction, is deployed without

awareness of its underlying logic, is qualitatively the same in every individual, and is distinct from more general abilities to process information or behave intelligently.

(Pinker 1994: 18)

Stevens' argument from this comparison is that as there are many rhythmic and sound-based similarities between music and language, there are potentially many areas where teaching approaches and activities can be linked. Poetry is one of these. Returning to Abbs, consider this statement about how music and poetry can inspire one another:

The music of poetry has the power to free language from its general bureaucratic servitude to literal meaning and one dimensional denotation. It opens language to the innate creativity of the speculative and questing mind and makes it a prime agent of exploration.

(Abbs 2003: 13)

We will be returning to the links between poetry and music within the *Dunwich Revisited* case study that forms a major part of this chapter. But whilst we are briefly considering the developmental aspects of language acquisition, it is worth pausing to consider the links to the visual arts. For young children, language development is often prefigured by the visual, as a flick through any young children's books will confirm. As Stevens comments, 'for the vast majority of young children, picture books prefigure purely written texts, and the attraction of seeing pictures mingling with words – in a huge and ever-expanding series of contexts – I suspect never leaves us' (Stevens 2011 110). Berger's work (1972) is another example of these links between language and the visual:

Seeing comes before words. The child looks and recognises before it can speak. But there is also another sense in which seeing comes before words. It is seeing which establishes our place in the surrounding world; we explain that world with words, but words can never undo the fact that we are surrounded by it.

(Berger 1972: 7)

So, the links between language development and the arts exist at a deep level, perhaps even informing each other in key biological and psychological ways. The following reflective task asks you some key questions that relate specifically to your own curriculum area.

Reflective task

What is the role of language within your subject? How does it affect the ways in which you plan for teaching your subject? Are there natural language abilities or attributes that pupils bring with them to your classroom that you can build on? Are there developmental processes in early childhood that might affect your approach here?

This chapter's aim is to explore how, building on these firm foundations, language can help underpin new approaches to cross-curricular teaching and learning in the arts. It will do this by considering how language and communication within the arts is distinctive from other areas of the curriculum, provide examples of approaches from the authors' work that illustrate key points and, finally, explore an approach to the use of metaphors which, it is hoped, will provide a useful tool for arts educators looking to develop cross-curricular approaches within and between their teaching.

But before we consider any of these things, it is useful to start with a broader consideration of how language relates to thinking within the arts. By doing this we hope to establish a platform from which more specific ideas can be developed.

Language and Thinking Within the Arts

Traditional views to the relationship between language and thinking suggest that they are inseparable elements of the same whole:

> When we adopt the monistic standpoint, we reject the claim that language and thinking can exist separately and independently of one another. Of course, we are talking about specifically *human* thinking, in other words about *conceptual* thinking. Thus we assert that in the process of cognition and communication, thinking and using a language are inseparable elements of one and the same whole.
>
> (Schaff 1973: 118)

There are many that challenge this claim. Polanyi's famous assertion that 'we know more than we can tell' (Polanyi 1967: 4) has been a resounding cry amongst arts educators. What he calls 'tacit knowledge' contains a range of conceptual and sensory information that allows us to make sense of things. In an inspirational chapter entitled 'Celebration of Thinking', Elliot Eisner picks up this thought and develops a sophisticated argument for a broader understanding of how thinking develops and relates to broader educational processes. Like Stevens (2011), Abbs (1982) and Pinker (1994) he cites the biological basis for thinking and learning within a broad assertion that 'brains are born and minds are made' (Eisner 1987: 2). Through this, he challenges the traditional, Platonic dichotomy of mind and body and asserts the development of a wider range of what he calls 'sensibilities' (ibid.), by which we are able to perform two very important cognitive operations: remembering and imagining. These, Eisner argues, can remain at the level of internal cognitive processes (i.e. they remain within our heads); to externalise these, we need forms of representation:

> Forms of representation are visual, auditory, tactile, gustatory and even olfactory. They manifest themselves in pictures, speech, the movements of dance and gesture, in words and in number. Each of these social devices carries meanings that represent qualities we have experienced directly or through recall or imagination.
>
> (Eisner 1987: 3)

These forms of representation will each have their own structures and promote a certain form of arrangement within their form, i.e. letters have to be arranged correctly to form words; visual elements within a painting such as line or form have to be arranged so that they cohere; movements within a dance relate to stylistic assumptions or conditions, etc. As can be seen by briefly considering these examples, the impact of external rules on these processes will vary. There will be more licence given to personal expression within the activity of painting that there would be to spelling (Rico (1983) explores this distinction in more detail).

This brief exposition of Eisner's riposte to the traditional assertion that language and thinking are inseparable serves as an important prelude to a key point in this chapter which seeks to examine the role of language in cross-curricular approaches to teaching and learning in the arts. That is, that a cross-curricular approach to language in the arts will require us to rethink what we mean by 'language' within our schools. The following extended quotation from Eisner's celebration of thinking says it most eloquently:

> A model of curriculum that exploits various forms of representation and that utilizes all of the senses helps students learn what a period in history feels like. Reality, whatever it is, is made up of qualities: sights, smells, images, tales, and moods. First-hand experience is simply a way of getting in touch with reality. In our schools we often rely upon conceptually dense and emotionally eviscerated abstractions to represent what in actuality is a rich source of experience.
>
> The hegemony of language on our curriculum and a narrow version at that, limits what students can come to know and restricts thinking processes to those mediated mainly by language. What language can carry is not all that we can know. Ultimately, what we know is rooted in qualities encountered or images recalled and imagined.
>
> (Eisner 1987: 4)

Eisner's argument rests on several key points that are worth briefly summarising here. First, that the various forms of representation by which we make sense of the world need to be part of every curriculum subject. The forms of representation need to be broad but also authentic and meaningful within that subject's culture and history. Limiting a subject to a particular, artificial form of representation is counterproductive, creates a false representation of that subject within the pupil's wider experience of the world and results in a false dichotomy in their understanding.

Second, the use of alternative forms of representation within your subject will, perhaps, make ideas and concepts easier to grasp for your pupils. Since Eisner wrote these paragraphs (over twenty years ago), the environment that young people grow up in has changed beyond recognition. The rich, visual and interactive environment of modern day communication channels is having a profound effect on young people's psychological, physiological and cognitive development that, as educators, we ignore at our peril. Some of the issues will be explored in the following chapter.

Finally, Eisner reasserts the view that language, although a powerful tool and an important one that, helps us remember and imagine, does not allow us to carry, or demonstrate, all that we know. As we will see in Chapter 6, the processes of assessment and educational evaluation will need to adapt accordingly if the fullness of pupils' learning in a cross-curricular context is to be uncovered.

Practical task

Make a list of the various 'forms of representation' that are contained within your subject area. Over the next few days find an example of each form of representation drawn from your pupils' work. If possible, ask a colleague who is working in a companion arts subject to do the same.

Individually, or working with your partner, consider the following questions in relationship to the work you have collected:

1. How is 'thinking' embodied or represented within the 'form of representation' that you have collected?

2. Is that 'thinking' something that the pupil has been able to articulate in other ways (i.e. through communication with you, through an evaluation of their work, discussion with other pupils, etc.)?

3. To what extent does the form of representation show things that the pupil cannot express in more traditional language forms?

4. Is there evidence of 'ways of thinking' from outside your arts subject that have been brought to bear on the pupils' work as represented in the objects you have collected?

Case Study – Dunwich Revisited

The following case study is drawn from one of the author's work (Savage and Challis 2001) at a high school in rural Suffolk. It has been chosen for inclusion within this chapter because it demonstrates effectively many of the points made in the discussion above about language, thinking and the role of the arts. It also helpfully moves our focus explicitly to issues associated with cross-curricular teaching and learning and the role of language within this.

The case study was a pivotal moment for the author concerned. It was initiated and sustained through a close working professional relationship with one of the mathematics teachers (Mike Challis) at the school who, coincidentally, was also studying for a PhD at the same university department as the author. At an artistic level, Challis' own musical work and involvement was central to the success of the project which was conducted, almost entirely, within the curriculum time allocated to music teaching with the school. This case study is lengthier than some of the others throughout the book. The reasons behind this choice will become clear as the discussion following it unfolds.

A new world is coming
And we don't know
Just where we're going next.

The old world is gone
And never to be found.
The past is in the past.

So say your prayers and say goodbye,
Say goodbye.

(Song composed by a group of Year 8 girls
within their music lesson as part of *Dunwich Revisited*)

This case study shares ideas, images, thoughts and judgements about a curriculum project, *Dunwich Revisited*, which took place at Debenham High School during January to March 2000. Through a description of the project and a sharing of the case study data, the events that took place within the classroom sessions, the extra-curricular rehearsals and, finally, on the concert hall stage will be discussed.

Situated on the east coast of Suffolk, the former city of Dunwich has had a rich and interesting history. During the early part of the second millennium it became a major port enjoying considerable wealth and prosperity. But due to the changing coastline, the emergence of a new river mouth further up the coast, and the silting up of its own port, Dunwich lost its place as the premier port on the east coast. Its source of prosperity was removed and the city itself eroded. During the next few hundred years most of the city was subsumed by the sea. Early last century All Saint's Church, at one time the largest church in Dunwich, gradually fell from the top of the cliffs into the sea. Photographs of this event taken over a period of time provided a major stimulus to the project. Visitors to Dunwich today will find a beautiful beach, sandy cliffs and the odd fishing shack.

The story of Dunwich has become a rich source of inspiration for poets, artists and composers. In 1989, Mike Challis, a local composer and teacher of mathematics at the high school, was asked to compose a piece of music to accompany a dance, 'States of Sea', to be performed by Splinters Youth Dance Group at Snape Maltings Concert Hall. This piece, called *Dunwich*, represented the changing landscape of Dunwich through its ternary (arch) shape. The opening section depicted the natural environment of the landscape that became Dunwich. The second section described the conquering of the natural forces of the environment and subsequent human inhabitation (through two medieval-like dance melodies). The final section portrayed the powerful natural elements reclaiming and overcoming these human interactions (in a return to the opening music).

In documentation made available to pupils during the *Dunwich Revisited* project, the choreographer of 'States of the Sea', Pamela Harling-Challis, Mike Challis' wife, wrote about the initial inspiration for her dance and the accompanying music:

> I grew up in a desert, a kind of sea filled with waves of sand, howling wind, masses of sky and immense distance. 'States of the Sea' is about a desert, where water comes between sand and sky. It is about time, change and the relentless pressure of the elements.

> The desert, the sea, the imagery of the Beaufort Scale, Dunwich Heath and the photographic remains of All Saints Church are all sources of inspiration.

Many of these things became inspirations for the pupils as they began to think about how they could reinterpret the story of Dunwich for themselves.

Mike Challis' composition *Dunwich* became the focus for a composition project involving the whole of the Years 7, 8 and 9, about 230 pupils in total, and the GCSE music group in Year 10 (15 pupils). Pupils were introduced to the place of Dunwich and its history before listening to the original piece. They were asked to make a series of responses to Challis' music, considering the mood, atmosphere and emotion of its various sections. The responses from each class formed part of a large wall display that later became a focus for an exchange of ideas and starting points for composition work. Pupils were then asked to spend time considering what type of sounds they might want to include in their own musical interpretation of Dunwich's history. They were encouraged to think of sounds that could be produced through using conventional instruments, voices, various technologies, or by selecting samples of environmental sounds that could be digitally imported into their piece.

Subsequent lessons involved pupils choosing ideas from these sheets and composing short sound ideas. Pupils made these ideas using a variety of technologies. The primary method was the use of a microphone connected to a simple sound processor/monitor set-up. Pupils experimented with various instrumental or vocal sound sources applying different types of effect to create the desired mood and atmosphere.

In addition to this way of working, other pupils in my GCSE class recorded environmental sounds on a portable Minidisc player. These sounds were then imported into a computer running a digital audio mixing programme (ProTools) before being edited using different pieces of computer software such as SoundHack, SoundEffects and Metasynth. All of these sound ideas were collected on the Minidisc player and carefully labelled in preparation for the next stage of the project. These sound ideas would eventually form the sonic material for pupils' own Dunwich pieces.

As well as the individual class pieces that the pupils produced, an open session was held during lunchtime to select sound ideas for a whole school performance piece. This piece would be played at Snape Maltings Concert Hall as part of the annual Suffolk Celebration of Schools' Music. This annual event is intended to provide a platform for pupils' performance and composition work. It is a non-competitive music festival with entries from primary and high schools around Suffolk.

All pupils involved in the project were invited to come and 'audition' each of the short sound ideas. Using a series of simple star ratings, the forty-five pupils who volunteered voted on which sounds they considered the most imaginative and appropriate for inclusion in this final piece. Out of 108 short sound ideas, twenty-four received five or more three-star votes. These sounds were to become the principal sonic material for the live performance piece. A group of thirty-five pupils, some volunteers and some selected, played in this performance and rehearsals began as an extra-curricular activity.

After the democratic selection of the various sound ideas to be included in the piece, lunchtime rehearsals enabled the various sections to be assembled. Work on the instrumental and vocal parts was carried out at the same time as the assembly of computer-generated sounds and the DJ elements of the piece. The ternary structure of the original *Dunwich* piece was used, with particular attention being paid to the transition points between sections. The 'merging' together of the various ideas involved considerable discussion between pupils, Mike Challis and myself. We were both keen to ensure that pupils had the final say as to what particular sound idea would go where in the final 'mix'. When there were disagreements between pupils, we acted as mediators and attempted to facilitate a reconciliation. This seldom happened and we were pleased to note that in the final project evaluation the pupils rated their sense of ownership in respect of the final product very highly.

During these lunchtime rehearsals a number of pupils began to think about the presentational side of the piece. They expressed concerned that the visual impact of the piece could be limited within a large concert hall space. They undertook to enhance the musical composition in two ways:

1.   Through the preparation of a large collage that would be constructed in real-time as the music played (see Figure 4.1);
2.   Through choreographing a dance to accompany the final two sections of the musical composition (portraying the human inhabitation of Dunwich and its eventual decline; see Figure 4.2).

Both of these additional elements were pursued by groups of pupils over the following weeks. It was exciting to see the purposeful and natural way that pupils worked across the often well-differentiated arts subject boundaries as the concert date got nearer.

Figure 4.1 Preparing the collage in rehearsals.

Figure 4.2 Dance rehearsals.

In the final week of the project the head teacher agreed to set aside two mornings for full rehearsals. These consisted of one hour for technical set up and then two hours of rehearsal and performance. The second rehearsal was on the day of the performance so all leads and inputs could be labelled and the entire set-up checked before leaving school. Pupils were made responsible for their part of the set-up to ease reassembly and disassembly at the concert hall. Careful consideration of the technical set-up was vital to ensure that technical hitches did not hold up the performance process. By labelling and rehearsing this part of the technical set-up pupils were able to set-up and perform the ten-minute piece twice within the forty-minute rehearsal slot at the concert hall. An audio and video recording of the final performance at Snape Maltings is included on the accompanying CD along with photographs of the final rehearsal and performance.

In addition to all of the above activities, in the remaining curriculum-based class sessions pupils were placed in different groups in order to share their various sound ideas. Each group composed their own piece using a selection of technologies, conventional instruments and voices. Using a series of compositional metaphors displayed on a specially constructed wall display, pupils focused on the idea of transition points combining the sound ideas into the larger ternary structures. Pupils were challenged to make the musical content of each section as original as possible.

The story of *Dunwich Revisited* is revealing in a number of aspects. It demonstrates key approaches to the use of language as a medium through which cross-curricular approaches to teaching and learning in the arts can be developed.

1. Start with the language of the artist

The language of the artist is a key starting point for anyone working within the arts. It is therefore a logical place to start when one is looking to broaden one's teaching through a cross-curricular approach. *Dunwich Revisited* drew explicitly on the work of two artists: first, Mike Challis' musical composition (*Dunwich*) which acted as a model for the pupils' own exploratory work, and was also used to shape and frame their work together within a final musical ternary form; second, the reflections of Pamela Harling-Challis, a local choreographer, on the process of piecing together a dance that reflected Dunwich Heath was another key stimulus for the pupils' work. Harling-Challis' own use of poetry, photographic and scientific materials also became of interest to the pupils, inspiring a sense of metaphorical play and a development of musical, and other, materials. Poetry also played an important role, with poems by local poets such as ex-pupil Paul Roberts being particularly appreciated by pupils.

2. Develop language within broad curriculum contexts

Alongside the obvious artistic context provided by the work of a composer, choreographer and poets, *Dunwich Revisited* built on a number of other contexts which relate clearly to other subjects within the National Curriculum. First, there was the environmental context which might help geographical knowledge and awareness. Many of the pupils knew about Dunwich. They had visited the coastline itself and explored its various elements. They had studied coastal erosion, something that is a current concern for much of the East Anglian coastline, and were familiar with how the coastline today has changed significantly in recent history.

Second, the historical context was important. Pupils had studied the history of the 1832 Reform Act which abolished the rotten boroughs. Up until that time, despite being underwater, Dunwich had returned two Members of Parliament to Westminster! People would travel to Dunwich, take a boat out to where (roughly) the town hall used to be and cast their vote there (see Suffolk Churches 2010 for further information on Dunwich and its history).

Culturally, the story of Dunwich and its associated myths and folklore was something that many pupils had heard. The idea of standing on the cliffs at midnight with a full moon and hearing the bells toll from the numerous Dunwich churches certainly caught their imagination. Seeing and hearing from the artists first-hand how these contexts had affected existing art works became an important stimulus for their own artistic processes and thinking.

3. Value the pupils' language

One of the key working principles within *Dunwich Revisited* was to place a strong degree of emphasis on the pupils' own artistic expression, their developing artistic language. Despite the decision to present pupils with a wide-ranging amount of initial stimulus materials, as well as an overall ternary structure for the final performance piece, pupils felt that it was a strong expression of their own emotions and feelings for the place of Dunwich.

> Everyone had the chance to contribute. The piece was different and individual. We composed it and no one had heard it before.
>
> (Anna, Year 8, in interview)

> I liked how original and contemporary it is. I mean, there is no other piece quite like it and you could never play the exact same piece again.
>
> (Carla, Year 9, in interview)

In this sense, the framework that underpinned pupils' work within *Dunwich Revisited* acted like a doorway through which they were empowered to create a language of expression that drew on a range of art forms. Wiggins (2003) picks up this metaphor in her work when she comments that:

> Finding a 'doorway in' is a metaphor designed to help teachers plan instruction to enable students to truly develop a structural understanding of music - an understanding that will empower their ability to listen to, perform, and create music, and enrich their capacity to understand what the music expresses.
>
> (Wiggins 2003)

What is true for music here, is also the case for all other arts subjects.

4. Value the natural emergence of cross-curricular links

Although *Dunwich Revisited* was initially conceived as a musical project, it quickly became cross-curricular in its scope. Pupils responded to the ideas being presented and used them to develop a language of expression that spanned many art forms, including music, dance, poetry and the visual arts. On reflection, it seems that the process of starting with the language of the artist itself, developing the broad curriculum contexts alongside this in the early stages of the project, and of valuing the language of the pupils, facilitated, for many involved, a natural engagement with cross-curricular ways of thinking. Although *Dunwich Revisited* was developed almost entirely through the curriculum time available for Key Stage 3 music within the school, together with some related extra-curricular activities, there were a number of examples of pupils making these links quite naturally. These were very exciting and resulted, we believe, in a commitment to this way of working that has led to these publications.

The first of these developments happened early on in the project. The words that were written by a group of Year 8 pupils (see the very opening of the case study) became an integral component for a song which formed the centrepiece of the final performance. The language of poetry, as noted by Abbs (2003: 3) is closely related to the language of music. Second, during the contemporary dance track performed by a DJ which formed part of the middle section of the piece, pupils were concerned that the performance lacked visual impact. They were quick to suggest the inclusion of dance which, as they commented, 'added an extra ingredient to the piece; it made the piece stand out and made the audience look up and think of the three Dunwich stages shown' (Sue, Year 9). (See Figure 4.3.)

Figure 4.3 Dancers in the final performance at Snape Maltings.

Pupils were also quick to ascribe a meaning to such an activity:

> It brought the mixing alive and represented fun and enjoyment during the daytime in Dunwich.
>
> (Claire, Year 8, in interview)

> The dancers represented human activity and life, whereas the first and last sections represented nature on its own.
>
> (Chloe, Year 10, in interview)

Finally, alongside the musicians and singers a collage was assembled, piece by piece, as the performance took place (see Figure 4.1).

It is important to stress that the inclusion of poetry and songwriting, dancing and the accompanying collage were ideas generated by the pupils themselves. To conclude this discussion of *Dunwich Revisited*, the following extract from the journal kept by the teacher involved in running the project re-emphasises some of the points made above:

> The naturalness in which the pupils made connections across the art forms is a real challenge to my way of thinking. The nature and structure of the curriculum within our high school does not actively facilitate the making of these links across the arts curriculum. In many respects the boundaries are well and truly established and maintained. But in contrast to this, pupils were more than happy to translate their ideas within a number of differing artistic contexts with great success. I believe this happened because in their wider lives pupils do not isolate artistic practices into discrete units of experience.

Reflective task

The *Dunwich Revisited* case study and following analysis has presented a pathway towards the development of a cross-curricular way of working and associated artistic, expressive language. Its four steps are:

- Start with the language of the artist;
- Develop language within broad curriculum contexts;
- Value the pupils' language;
- Value the natural emergence of cross-curricular links.

It is never a good idea to copy other teachers. The purpose in discussing *Dunwich Revisited* is not so that it can be copied and taught elsewhere.

Rather, use it and the accompany analysis as a tool to reflect on your own teaching. What can it help you learn about:

1. How you design a curriculum project of your own to encourage pupils in the development of a cross-curricular language?

2. How you use and position the work of artists as a stimulus for developing pupils' own expressive voices?

3. How you can build on pupils' natural interests in linking together their learning in various art subjects, and beyond these to other areas of the curriculum?

4. The extent to which cross-curricular projects of this type need to be the result of collaborations between subjects. To what extent can cross-curricular approaches to teaching and learning in the arts be applied within your own teaching and within your own curriculum time? Is a cross-curricular approach to teaching and learning in the arts solely about collaboration? Or is it about your own pedagogy?

Having considered an example of a piece of curriculum development within the arts, we will now turn our attention to the use of a specific language 'tool' or 'type' which, we will argue, will help you begin to plan for a more cross-curricular approach within your own teaching.

Developing metaphors as a tool for cross-curricular language

Metaphors are a language 'type' that has some potential in helping teachers make links across traditional subject cultures. Lakoff and Johnson (1981: 5) define a metaphor as: '... understanding and experiencing one kind of thing in terms of another'. This definition is built on the notion of a metaphor being able to capture the essential nature of a particular experience and relating it to something else. We have already explored Anna Sfard's metaphors for learning in Chapter 3. For our purposes, metaphors are a perfect type of language for our discussion about cross-curricular pedagogy within the arts. 'Understanding' (again, see Chapter 3) and 'experiencing' are also active words that resonate strongly with processes underpinning Eisner's argument (Eisner 1987) for multiple forms of representation and knowing that we also explored at the beginning of this chapter. In another key similarity with Eisner, Lakoff and Johnson insist that metaphors are not solely based in language. Metaphors, in their definition, can include any expression or thing that is symbolic for a person. This would include non-verbal behaviours, pieces of artwork or something in a person's imagination. In other words, anything a person sees, hears, does, feels or imagines can be used to help them think or reason through metaphor:

> In all aspects of life, ... we define our reality in terms of metaphors and then proceed to act on the basis of the metaphors. We draw inferences, set goals, make commitments,

and execute plans, all on the basis of how we in part structure our experience, consciously and unconsciously, by means of metaphor.

(Lakoff and Johnson 1981: 158)

Again, this situates the use of metaphors as a 'tool' for teaching and learning well within our remit as teachers of the arts. It also presents us with an opportunity to explore a new approach from which teachers in other curriculum subjects and areas can learn.

The use of metaphors as tools for teaching and learning have a long history. According to Gorden (1978), one can chart the use of metaphor (and the related concept of analogy which, he suggests, is merely an extended metaphor) back to Greek myths, religious texts and fairy tales which all help readers (or listeners) learn expected conduct. Hoffman (1983) estimated that the average English-speaker uses over 3,000 metaphors every week as part of their natural language use, and Bowers (1993) goes as far as suggesting that all human thinking is metaphorical in some way. It is interesting to reflect for a moment on the number of metaphors that relate to learning itself (e.g. switching on a light bulb, planting a seed, etc.).

According to the Lakoff and Johnson definition, metaphors describe one experience in terms of another. As a teaching and learning tool, a metaphor can help the teacher relate something unfamiliar to pupils with something familiar. This gets to the Greek root of the word metaphor (metapherein) which means to transfer. Metaphors can also be used to specify and constrain our ways of thinking about the original experience. This influences the meaning and importance one can attach to the original experience, the way it fits with other experiences, and the actions that one can take as a result. Pedagogically, this may or may not be problematic. Glynn and Takahashi (1998) warn that metaphors need to be handled carefully within educational situations. Incorrect use of metaphors can lead to greater confusion. Teachers must make sure that the coherence of the metaphor is accurate and clear. There is a responsibility for the teacher, within the classroom setting, of choosing the appropriate metaphor and using it in a way that promotes clear communication.

Water's work on productive metaphors (Waters 1994) underpinned the work that pupils did within the *Dunwich Revisited* project. Water's work has been discussed at length in the companion title to this series (Savage 2011) but is revisited here, more briefly, within the context of the arts. Early experiments with these productive metaphors underpinned an approach to the teaching of musical composition with Key Stage 3 pupils prior to the *Dunwich Revisited* project (see Savage 1999 for further information). Part of this involved the construction of a wall-display of metaphors under various headings that Waters had developed within what he called a 'toolbox of productive metaphors' (Waters 1994: 75).

Water's study of metaphors centred on art-making processes in various digital arts fields. But, as we will consider, these can be usefully applied to the context of cross-curricular teaching and learning within the arts. His 'Toolbox of Productive Metaphors' is divided into four main sections:

- Basic Concepts
- Strategies of Connection
- Strategies of Reduction
- Strategies of Contextualisation

Although he acknowledges that these distinctions are artificial, this four-part structure does represent a helpful framework within which the metaphors can be explored. Water's work (ibid.) is extensive in this regard but, for our purposes, in each section below we have chosen two metaphors to explore briefly. Each metaphor is presented and defined through a quotation from Waters' work. Following this, we have added our own interpretation of the metaphor that, we hope, will prove helpful to your own work in applying metaphors to the teaching of your own arts subject in the following practical task. These personal, and hopefully artistic, interpretations of the metaphor may contain examples of ideas of how the metaphor might be represented (within particular subjects), questions about the metaphor and how it might be interrogated to produce links between subjects, or just immediate, reflective responses to the possibility of the metaphor and its application to pedagogy. They are by no means conclusive (so please do not read them as such), and are merely included to help prompt your own thinking about how the metaphor can help you understand or experience one thing in terms of another. In Water's own words:

> What is offered here is a toolbox of productive metaphors; keywords which are not in any current sense discipline-specific, although they have originated in a specific practice. ... They are all intended as projects for further investigation and personal annotation. The incompleteness are therefore intentional; an invitation to continue, to add, to argue.

> (Waters 1994: 75–6)

1. Basic concepts

Resolution/definition

> The resolution of an experience or a system is the relation of the size of its components to that of the whole. In a high resolution experience, the grain or individual elements of the representational medium chosen do not impinge on the definition or distinctiveness of the represented object.

> (Waters 1994, pp.78-9)

Resolution/definition is about a relationship between individual components and the whole. It could relate to geographical elements such as maps or photographs which contain numerous graphical or actual elements that relate together to form a landscape or ecosystem; there are artistic dimensions such as the choice of colours and their interaction in a painting; it could be translated to the way in which we view particular objects, events or time periods in a historical narrative, focusing in on particular moments or zooming out to capture wider societal, political or cultural movements. Zooming could become a productive metaphor in its own right. Microscopes zoom in and out on things providing greater or lesser definition of an object. Narrative structures within poetry allowing the writer to zoom in on a particular object, event or person, describing it in greater detail and enhancing its meaning when compared to the surrounding text. When digitally recorded, sounds can be microanalysed and you often notice things that you missed first time around. Backgrounds become foregrounds; foregrounds become backgrounds. Suddenly, perspective gets confused. As artists, are we wanting to control what our audience can see or hear? As audience, are we looking in the right place or listening in the right way? Does it matter?

Play

> Play in its many forms is one of the closest forms of performance activity. Yet such exploratory behaviour is undervalued and suppressed in most areas of human activity beyond childhood.
>
> (Waters 1994: 80)

Does your subject encourage a sense of play? What would this involve? What is playfulness and how does it relate to learning? Are some pupils, or subjects, more playful than others? If play is undervalued and suppressed within education, how could the arts seek to value and utilise it more? If play involves making mistakes and failing, how can I teach my pupils to fail well? What would they learn from that? If playful learning is the answer, what is the question? (Heppell 2010).

2. Strategies of Reduction

Editing

> Editing is selecting, moving things around, deleting or erasing, cutting and pasting.
>
> (Waters 1994: 83)

As an artistic process, editing is a vital skill. It applies to every curriculum area but is something that needs to be encouraged because it seems, from our experience, that pupils like to avoid it. In our discussions of the creative process in Chapter 2 we discussed the importance of revision, and editing is another facet of this. Pupils like to produce things; perhaps the sense of achievement is tied up in the final object that they produce? Perhaps editing is misread as failure? How can this process be slowed down so that the pathway towards the final object of their learning is appreciated more fully? How can editing be encouraged as part of a playful process of engagement within my subject? How can I keep the opportunities and options for choices open for longer rather than forcing pupils down a particular route (perhaps for expediency or to save time)? Within the arts, what are the devices that we can adopt and share to encourage the process to be savoured and appreciated more fully?

Iteration

> Iteration is a strategy for moving towards a required goal as quickly as possible. It relies on repeatedly attempting whatever is being done, and selecting those outcomes which most closely meets the goal.
>
> (Waters 1994: 85)

Iterative processes can be found in various curriculum areas. Mathematicians use iterative processes to help in averaging and estimating; scientists use them to help generate hypotheses; artists sketch and doodle; musicians jot ideas down through improvisations. Repeatedly attempting something is not worthless activity in and of itself, providing it becomes part of a creative and intellectual process. It creates mental and physical patterns that become part of how we act, think or feel within an activity. How can all this be valued more? From the pupils' perspective, perhaps the problems associated with iteration are similar to those related to editing? Can they learn to value this process too?

3. Strategies of connection

Diffusion

> Diffusion is the activity which results in an object or behaviour becoming more widespread that previously. It is also a metaphor of the increasing social connection or dissemination of a process.
>
> (Waters 1994: 87)

My first thought here is of gases. They diffuse under certain conditions. But other things diffuse too. I have an image of ripples on a pond, diffusing outwards towards the edge; sound diffuses differently depending on the acoustic properties of a space. Is it about multiplication in some sense? But it could also be about replacement, because sometimes the thing that is diffused changes so much that nothing of the original source is left behind (at least, not in our consciousness). Replacement might be another productive metaphor worth exploring. There is a creative link here to iteration and patterning. Both these are vital activities in every art form. What links could we make?

Mapping

> In addition to the widely understood cartographical sense of making a representation of a geographical surface, indicating its features, there is an equally significant metaphorical sense of the term from mathematics, this referring to the association of each element of one system or set with that from another system or set.
>
> (Waters 1994: 87)

In an obvious sense, mapping something involves investigating it thoroughly and representing it in a particular form. In another sense, it is about translation, taking the properties or proportions of one structure and using them to determine the structure of something else. Therefore, the mathematical results of an equation might be used to determine a new type of musical scale; the contour analysis of a particular land-form becomes a starting point for a piece of art. What 'maps' could be exchanged between the arts? What would that picture sound like? What would that composition look like? What historical approaches to the mapping of arts processes could we borrow from? What would Laban Movement Analysis look like if it was translated from dance into music? What would that dance 'sound' like if I performed and captured it digitally and converted it using light beam technologies? What new type of expressive language would result in that process?

4. Strategies of contextualisation

Reading/interpretation

> An extended sense of the term 'reading' can be usefully related to an extended sense of the work 'text'. In acknowledgement of the cultural and historical contingency of

any 'reading', such 'readings' are regarded as being in contention, completing for attention. In practice, most individuals tend to favour what is experientially a single, albeit continuously evolving, sense of what something means in order to be able to negotiate, at least temporarily, and share meanings with other people.

(Waters 1994: 89)

Reading is central to the majority of subjects. But common elements of reading get applied and reinterpreted within each subject. And we, as individuals, also read in different ways. We read or interpret a book, an image, a musical score, an advertisement. These all involve (and imply) different sets of skills and result in different understandings. One person's reading will vary from another. This is because we do not read or interpret something as a blank canvas. We contextualise what we read and interpret against our previous experiences. We have to negotiate and share our meanings of things to gain a consensus. Sometimes, a lack of consensus is the best outcome. It gives us our personality. So, what are the links between reading a text, an image, a film or a piece of music? What are the skills that underpin these related activities? We thought about the role of understanding in Chapter 3. As teachers, how are the processes that we undertake within our pedagogy to elicit and develop our pupils' understanding related? There is much of value here for a cross-curricular pedagogy perhaps.

Recontextualisation

Recontextualisation involves moving something from a position to which it, or those experiencing it, has become accustomed, to another position. Of course this position may be conceptual rather than spatial.

(Waters 1994: 90)

These books are about recontextualisation! As teachers, we have the power to move ideas around and this is one of the major challenges this series of books is promoting. It is also a key to this whole concept of productive metaphors acting as prompts for cross-curricular language development within the arts and your associated pedagogy. Specifically, what happens to a literature text when it is recontextualised within a different genre – the theatre, a film or musical? When objects are moved they take on a different dimension. 'Play Me, I'm Yours' shows this clearly. In this art project Luke Jerram relocated pianos within different urban environments (skate parks, bus stations, industrial estates) and left them there for the local communities to use as they saw fit (Jerram 2009). Pianos, once the object of the pianist, take on a different dimension as they are used in whatever way the local community wants. One specialist music school has bought a number of old pianos, and placed them in corridors, communal spaces and other non-classroom areas. They became the focus for informal music-making in all sorts of interesting ways. What would this look like for familiar objects within schools, within your classroom or other communal spaces? What impact would this have on pupils' learning inside and outside the classroom?

As a linguistic device, the metaphor is a powerful tool in linking together the content and pedagogy of different subject areas. The *Dunwich Revisited* case study was underpinned by pupils' working with metaphors of the type that Waters has explored and which we discussed above. Hopefully, as you have read through the eight metaphors described above possible ideas have been stimulated in your imagination. Hang on to these! You will need them for the following practical task.

In applying metaphors to develop cross-curricular approaches to teaching and learning, there are various methods to aid one's thinking. The approach that I am going to present here is paraphrased on a model produced by Eikenberry (2009) and adopted by the NASAGA (2009). Their 3C Model provides a helpful structure for applying metaphors to learning contexts. It is based on two premises. First, that the brain works by building connections and associations between concepts and ideas; second, that the brain remembers more easily things that are unusual or novel. The three-stage model incorporates the following three steps: Create, Connect and Combine. This model will be introduced in a practical task which will help you apply metaphors (either those drawn from Waters' work, described above or your own) to the teaching of a lesson that introduces a new concept to your pupils. It was first introduced in the companion title to this book (Savage 2011) but is adapted here for the context that you, as a teacher in the arts, will be facing.

Practical task

1. Create

    a. Determine which lesson you want to focus on. Make sure you allow yourself plenty of time to complete this element of the planning process.

    b. Write down all the key elements of the topic that you want to cover during the lesson. This would include trying to sketch out some key learning objectives and outcomes for the lesson.

    c. How do you want to teach this? Think about the type of teaching or learning activities that you might want to incorporate within the lesson. It would also include examples you might use in the explanatory parts of the lesson. Write down any ideas you have in simple, non-jargon, non-technical language. This will help you see potential metaphors more easily. You can afford to be quite experimental here. Do not rule out ideas at this stage. You may also want to think generally about the resources that you want to use, or explore, within the lesson and how these might affect the teaching and learning activities.

    d. At this point you are going to begin to compile a list of metaphors for use within the lesson. Go through the list of key elements that you have constructed. What do these remind you of? Use free association techniques to help here. How did you remember these elements when you were learning about them? This is a creative process and some of the ideas may be odd, strange or incomplete. This does not matter at the moment. Write them down anyway.

c. What could I do visually to enhance the connection between my content and the metaphor?

As mentioned in the previous answer, there are many options here. Using the wall space in the classroom can help (see Savage 1999 for one example of how this was done to good affect). Put up graphics or pictures of the metaphor or its component parts. Use a theme on any presentational and class materials that you prepare for the lesson to accentuate the metaphor.

d. What other senses can I use to solidify the metaphor?

Think about other senses beyond sight. How can pupils engage their sense of touch (perhaps through a model or toy), smell (actual or related), or hearing (sound effects, other noises). I remember watching a lesson about musical form which included binary, ternary and rondo forms (basically an AB, ABA and ABACA structure respectively). The trainee teacher bought this to life by making a basic hamburger in front of the class. Binary (AB) became the bottom half of the bun and the burger; ternary (ABA) placed the top of the bun on the top part of the burger; rondo form involved placing another burger and top part of the bun on top of the existing 'ternary' burger – it ended up looking like a Big Mac! I was not sure what it tasted like, but it smelt good and I am certain the pupils remembered their musical forms for a while.

e. How can I reinforce the metaphor in the conclusion of the lesson?

Make sure that you reinforce the metaphor through repetition at the end of the lesson, by referencing it in your plenary and using it to help structure questions that relate to the new content taught alongside the metaphor. Ask pupils to summarise the new content, using the metaphor and any associated frameworks as a guide.

Conclusion

This chapter began with an exploration of the links between the arts and language. Its main preoccupation has been with how pupils' expressive language, both verbal and artistic, can be developed through cross-curricular approaches to teaching and learning within the arts which, whilst remaining faithful to their individual subject cultures, allows for a natural playfulness on the part of the pupils (and, we hope, teachers) in forging cross-curricular links. Through a consideration of one piece of curriculum development, *Dunwich Revisited,* we explored a simple process by which this type of cross-curricular language development might be encouraged. This needs to be placed alongside some of the broader arguments within this book, and the companion title (Savage 2011), which explore in more detail aspects of your individual pedagogical elements which will also help facilitate this process. Finally, we considered the use of metaphors as an artistic tool to help forge links between different ways of making or playing within the arts. These, it was suggested, have a rich potential for new pieces of curriculum development that prioritise cross-curricular ways of working both within your own teaching, and more broadly in collaborative ventures with other colleagues. In all of this, we have forged a close link to our colleagues in the Humanities where, it seems, there is a similar embracing of the interdisciplinary potential of language as a medium for artistic endeavour. Stevens' book (Stevens 2011) puts it most eloquently:

> Effectively, in this book I attempt to argue for a new kind of English teacher: an interdisciplinary English teacher, aware of the breadth of the subject and the interconnectivities involved (the *inter* of 'interdisciplinary', which is why I prefer the term to 'cross-curricular'), but also especially conscious of *language*, in all its textual diversity, as the sharp focus. Certainly few throughout the world of education would disagree that a secure grasp of language and its qualities lies at the heart of effective teaching and learning – and this is the very stuff, the defining characteristic, of English in the curriculum.
>
> (Stevens 2011: 3)

What is true for the written and spoken language is true for the many types of expressive and artistic languages that we are wanting our pupils to develop. And for us as teachers the same argument applies, we believe, for this book and the new generation of teachers of the arts that we hope it will inspire.

Professional Standards for QTS

This chapter will help you meet the following Q standards: Q4, Q17, Q23, Q25c.

Professional Standards for Teachers

This chapter will help you meet the following core standards: C4, 7, 29d.

The cross-curricular potential of technology within the arts

Key objectives

By the end of this chapter, you will be able to:

- Analyse the contribution technology makes to processes of cross-curricular teaching and learning within the arts.

- Make links between your own arts practices and your use of technology within the classroom.

- Reflect on various case studies of others' practices in these areas and draw lessons for your own professional development.

- Reflect on the future of cross-curricular arts education and the role that technology may play in this.

Introduction

Technology has permeated every aspect of our lives as artists in the early twenty-first century. It provides us with new opportunities to listen to music, create and manipulate visual materials, to produce and share artistic ideas, act, dance, play, teach and learn from each other. The use of technology in the arts subjects has challenged and reshaped views about the principles and purposes of arts teaching and learning. Whilst the same might be true in other areas of the curriculum, it seems fair to assume that within the arts the impact of technology has been particularly significant in respect of the cultural practices within the arts and the associated ways of knowing. This chapter will explore some of these key themes, and address what the arts can learn from each other in terms of their use of technology within cross-curricular approaches to teaching and learning.

Reflective task

As technology becomes more pervasive and allows us greater access to music from around the world, Bennett Reimer has wondered whether musical performance is worth saving as a key activity within music education (Reimer 1994; Savage 2005a). His provocative stance asks music teachers to question the precise skills, embodied knowledge or understanding that the activity of musical performance actually facilitates in an age where young people can access music through new technologies quickly and easily. Why do they need to play anymore? Within the United Kingdom this is something that is currently receiving considerable attention as approaches to whole-class instrumental teaching, such as Wider Opportunities, are embedded in Local Authorities across the country. The perceived benefits of this on students' self-esteem and wider academic studies are easily written about in evaluative studies (FMS 2010) but perhaps less easy to substantiate due to a lack of longitudinal studies in these areas (Savage 2010).

Reflect on this statement and compare it to the situation within your own subject area. Consider the following questions:

– How has technology made its mark within your subject area?
– Has it brought into question key ideas about how your subject is represented or how it engages students?
– Has this always had a positive impact from your point of view?
– How should we respond to the changing culture of our arts subjects in a digital age?

If you have time, find a colleague from another arts subject and ask them to reflect on these same questions. Compare your answers.

The first reflective task asked you to consider how technology leaves it mark on our work and in our minds; as teachers, its imprint becomes firmly embedded within our pedagogies, implicating our thinking in implicit and explicit ways. Once there, it is hard to remove, and the nature of our responses to it shape our conceptions about arts education. The same is true of our work as artists. It is often hard to remove the stamp that technology imprints on our work. Of course, this may or may not be desirable. That is part of the decision that artists make about their work and how they represent it.

But maybe you feel your work as a teacher has 'escaped' this technological imprint up to this point? I would gently like to question this assumption in two ways. First, all the arts depend on technology in one way or the other. Whilst the focus of this chapter is on the use of information and communication technologies (ICT), or what we might term 'digital technologies', for centuries artists have used various tools as means of expression. The choice and application of particular tools is an important part in an artist's practice. Using and abusing tools is a vital part of every artistic activity. Many musicians are fascinated by the working practices of visual artists. They often compare these to ways of working within musical composition. As an example, one television programme has recently involved an infamous 'forger' of oil paintings working with a range of celebrities in the recreation of famous scenes from the history of art. Whilst this might not seem to be a particularly creative activity in and of itself, it was surprising to see the full range of physical gestures that this particular artist made in recreating the work of a famous 'master' painter. These included using his hands and fingers in different ways, alongside his paint brush, and involved him scratching, flicking, jabbing and caressing the paint onto the canvas in a highly energetic way. This element of performance, of investing the raw materials of painting with acrylics with a naturalistic energy, was enlightening. It reminded us of experimental performance techniques with various instruments that we have observed whilst watching electro-acoustic composers working within recording studios. Traditional instrumental (or painting) tools and techniques will get you so far; finding alternative approaches to playing an instrument (or a canvas) can take you into new territories.

But our general point here is that as teachers working within the arts we have a long tradition of using technology in one form or another as an integral part of our creative practice. We should not ignore or forget this. The histories of our subjects and their established cultures can provide us with many clues as to how we should seek to implement newer types of technologies and use them to develop cross-curricular ways of working between ourselves and to make links with other curriculum areas.

Practical task

Make a list of all the 'technologies' that you use in your teaching. Include digital technologies and other traditional technologies that you might use (e.g. staff notation, palette knives, brushes etc.). For each tool, think about what it allows a pupil to achieve (i.e. what it 'affords'), as well as what it might inhibit within the artistic processes that underpin your subject.

Second, our work as teachers has not escaped technology's 'imprint' because of our students and the world that they inhabit. Their experience of the arts outside the formal learning context is often technologically rich in a multiplicity of ways. Learning in the 'real' world, outside of the formality of schools and classrooms, is often portrayed as transparent and boundless when compared to the formal classroom. Without the prevailing subject cultures and unhelpful categorisations of knowledge and pedagogy that dominate our schools, in the 'real' world learners can navigate their way seamlessly amongst and in-between subject knowledge that, the argument goes, they might find more difficult to achieve in a more formal setting. Of course, such bald parallels are based on false assumptions and a narrow understanding of what happens within both the classroom and the 'real' world. But the intelligent use and application of technologies has provided us with an opportunity to challenge our way of thinking about subjects, curricula, teaching and learning. Has this discourse really passed you by? To what extent has your work successfully responded to the technology's imprint on the artistic lives of your students?

Practical task

At the next appropriate opportunity, take some time in one of your lessons to explore these issues with your own pupils. As a start, why not ask them to make a list of the pieces of technology that they use regularly in their school and wider lives. These might include mobile phones, computers, pieces of software or web environments, social networking sites, computer tablets, etc. For each item, ask the pupils to list some of the main purposes or uses that they make from it. Ask them to try to relate some of the purposes to the subject area that you teach. You might be surprised at how many links there are. Finally, how do the lists they make compare to the list you put together in Practical Task 1?

The challenge of responding positively to the imprint of technology on the arts is not easy. There are many strong forces that militate against it. One of the restraining elements is a strong, traditional view of the arts within their particular subject cultures. For Goodson and Mangen, a 'subject culture' (Goodson and Mangen 1998: 120) is 'an identifiable structure which is visibly expressed through classroom organisation and pedagogical styles'. Elsewhere in this series of books (Savage 2011), we have explored how, for many teachers, the subject culture and its associated 'ways of being' (Van Manen 1977: 205) define their teaching practice at a fundamental level. In this book, we considered the notion of teacher identities in Chapters 1 and 3. Within the secondary education context, the opportunity to develop one's subject and teach others about it is high up the list of most teachers' job satisfaction (Spear *et al*. 2000: 52). Within initial teacher education, subject knowledge (i.e. the actual knowledge of the subject but also, implicitly, the way that the subject is presented and traditionally taught), is a strong, formative force on the beginner teacher. These elements in our work are powerful and, often, helpful in facilitating the process of learning to teach. But, left unchallenged, these can consolidate and congeal approaches to teaching and learning within the arts. One of the underpinning arguments of this book is that all teachers need to cultivate a deliberate sense of 'playful engagement' with their formative subject culture. Teachers within the arts subjects need to lead the way on this. The critical and reflective teacher of the arts stands a better chance of responding positively to the use of new technologies when they have been able to reconceptualise their subject culture to accommodate new technological-mediated artistic practices.

Developing cross-curricular approaches – teaching and learning in the arts through technology

As we have discussed above, technologies have formed part of artistic practice across the centuries. This basic fact should give us confidence in dealing with the new range of technologies that are available to us in the twenty-first century. Obviously, the technologies available today will change in dramatic ways over the next twenty years.

Some of these we may be able to predict; others will take us all by surprise. But the impact of these new technologies will be dependent upon the social context, value frameworks, educational agendas and pedagogies that they are brought into and work alongside them.

To illustrate this point, the following case study is drawn from Savage's work as a teacher at a small high school in rural Suffolk (Savage and Challis 2002). Since the case study was completed several years ago, the types of technologies available within schools have developed dramatically. But, as you read the case study, note the wider context within which these technologies were placed, and also the cross-curricular activities that this wider context facilitated.

CASE STUDY 1: Reflecting Others

Music lessons for pupils in Years 9 and 10 at Debenham High School were far from conventional during the Autumn 2000 and Spring 2001 terms. Within them you would have been as likely to find pupils working with digital video cameras, iMac computers, Minidisc players and microphones as with traditional classroom instruments. You would have found pupils recording the hustle and bustle of school life, the countryside, their hobbies and interests, collecting audio samples from CDs and radio programmes as well as visual images from the local skateboard park and leisure centre, all in relation to the project's themes of identity, community and environment. This material (over 20 gigabytes in total) was recorded onto a number of iMac computers before being edited and transferred to an external hard disk as a 'digital scrapbook'.

In another part of Suffolk, within a highly secure special unit at Her Majesty's Prison Hollesley Bay, young offenders were offered the opportunity to carry out a similar exercise. Both pupils and young offenders documented, through sonic and visual digital recordings, their environment, sense of identity and community as young, twenty-first century teenagers.

After a small amount of editing by project staff to remove the names of pupils and prisoners from some of these materials, the school and prison exchanged these 'digital scrapbooks' after Christmas. The exchanged digital scrapbook became source materials for a number of sonic and visual compositions each made by one group about the other. Pupils worked on the material collected by the young offenders; the young offenders worked on the material collected by the pupils. They selected, edited and manipulated the images and sounds using a variety of innovative software tools, including MetaSynth, Digital Performer and Adobe Premiere. Each of these pieces of software, despite being tools for professional use, proved easy to adapt for use within the classroom environment. The sonic and visual compositions produced were arranged to make a specially designed sound and visual installation that was housed in the Exhibition Room at Snape Maltings Concert Hall. The installation was transferred to the school and the prison before returning to Snape Maltings for public viewing during the 2001 Aldeburgh Festival and Snape Proms.

Key to the success of the project was the involvement of two artists: the electro-acoustic composer Mike Challis (employed as a teacher of mathematics at the school) and the filmmaker (employed by Aldeburgh Productions for the duration of the project). Both worked in the school and the prison, combining and sharing their technological skills and artistic awareness with classes of pupils and young offenders most effectively.

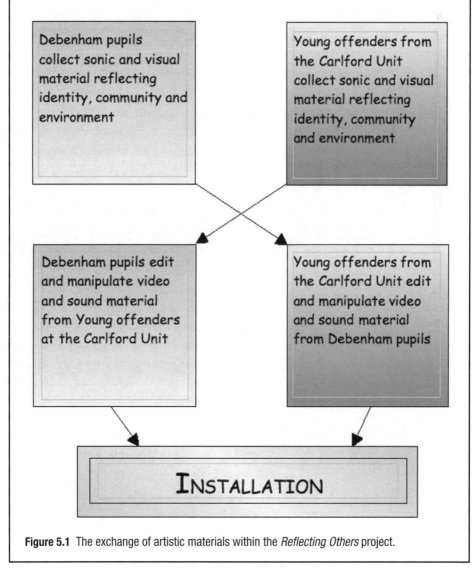

Figure 5.1 The exchange of artistic materials within the *Reflecting Others* project.

113

Reflective task

Whilst technologies have developed since the *Reflecting Others* case study, the requirement for teachers to be imaginative about the context for their use remains the same. Reflect on this case study through the following questions:

1. The three themes for the *Reflecting Others* project were identity, community and environment. Would these themes be suitable for a cross-curricular project of this type today?

2. Which of today's technologies could be used to facilitate a project of this type?

3. Within their music lessons, pupils were working on photographic, digital video and digital audio materials. What challenges does this broadening of activities make on a teacher? How could they be mitigated?

4. *Reflecting Others* was a collaboration between a local arts agency, a school and a local prison. It took place within the curriculum time allocated to one art's subject within the school but depended on this broader network. How could you seek to make use of technology to help broaden your network and provide a context for learning that spans out of the time that is allocated for the teaching of your subject within your school?

As technologies change, the development of cross-curricular approaches to using technology within the arts will make different demands on teachers. Making informed choices about which type of technologies to use is important. However, the wider curriculum within which these technologies are placed is equally important. Just having the technology in the classroom will not change very much in and of itself. The four principles outlined below will help you make informed choices about your use of technology and also help you develop a context for cross-curricular teaching and learning in conjunction with these technologies.

But before we consider these principles, it is vital to stress the importance of maintaining a critical stance in relationship to these issues and not succumbing to the false rhetoric that surrounds many of the debates about ICT in education. Technologies do not hold all the answers to the potential educational challenges that teachers within the arts will face. They are one part of a web of influences on their work. Their use is mediated by other important and powerful factors that need to be held within a careful balance. This chapter is an integral part of a book that espouses a particular cross-curricular approach to teaching and learning in the arts. Technology has a small part to play in this. But it is intimately and intricately linked to the broader set of ideas that this book contains.

The first reflective task within this chapter asked you to consider the role of key artistic processes that underpin your subject. Many of these will be key elements of your subject's culture and, if available, will be articulated within the Key Concept statements within your subject's Key Stage 3 National Curriculum documentation. These key concepts should not be undermined by technology. Rather, they should be enhanced.

The relationship between new pedagogical approaches that emerge through the use of technology within and between arts subjects will be a delicate and fragile one that needs to be understood and reflected on in two ways. First, you will want to reflect on this within the context of the subject itself. Second, any collaborative work between yourself and other arts colleagues will need to focus on the impact of new approaches on cross-curricular ways of teaching and learning between your subjects. An appropriate approach to educational evaluation will need to underpin these discussions. This approach reinforces the observation made by Lawrence Stenhouse, that 'there is no curriculum development without teacher development' (Stenhouse 1980: 85). This belief underpins the companion title in this series (Savage 2011) and is a key driver throughout all the series' titles. Teachers will by no means be redundant in technological future scenarios. Developing that reflective 'eye' and 'ear', and being alert to the changing nature of their pedagogy will be key skills, whatever new technologies may emerge.

With this in mind, this chapter will outline four key principles for arts educators as new technologies emerge and are applied to the processes of cross-curricular teaching and learning.

Principle 1: Technology and your artistic practice

In our view, all teachers of the arts should be practising artists of some sort. They should also value their subject cultures. Developing a cross-curricular approach within your teaching is not about trampling on and dismissing individual subject cultures. These contain sets of values, definitions and interests (Jephcote and Davies 2007: 210) that, although often hard to define, are experienced by participants within that culture almost intuitively. Our subject cultures frame, in a historical sense, the philosophy, practice and pedagogies of our subject and we ignore this at our peril. As we have discussed throughout this book, the arts subjects have significantly personal, emotive and aesthetic dimensions that are underpinned by ways of knowing and 'doing' that stretch back over many centuries. These infiltrate and inform the approach to teaching our subject in subtle ways. There are many links between arts subjects at this level. For example, many arts subjects emphasise the importance of the teacher working in the role as artist, musician or performer within the classroom. Although modelling is an important tool in every teacher's arsenal, it has a particular resonance for the active artist, musician, dancer or actor and their teaching.

Therefore, the first principle for arts teachers in their use of technology as a tool for cross-curricular teaching and learning is to be an informed user of technology within your specific art form itself. Please note here that we are not specifying here what types of technologies need to become central in your artistic practice. We are, obviously, making an assumption here that you are an active artist within your field. From that position of being immersed in the process of creation, evaluation and communication you will be using a range of technological tools. These will vary from pencils, paints, manuscript paper and other traditional items to, perhaps, the latest advances of digital technologies. Wherever your practice is at, having a strong and informed rationale for the choice and use of particular tools within your art form is an essential first step in the development of cross-curricular work.

From this position of strength, and from within the 'comfort' of your own subject culture, it is important to begin to explore the potential cross-curricular links that you can make in your own artistic practice. Here, ICT has a very important, simple and powerful role to play in allowing us to access ideas and develop our understanding of potential new approaches within our art form. The definition for a cross-curricular approach to teaching that we introduced in Chapter 1 emphasises that it is underpinned by a sensitivity towards and synthesis of knowledge, skills and understandings from various subject areas. There is no short cut here. Finding out about the artistic processes, uses of technology and underpinning rationales of subject cultures outside our own, and our neighbouring arts colleagues who represent them, will take time. But it will be time well spent.

Practical task

Commit to starting this process of enquiry and communication with other arts colleagues within your initial teacher education course or school as soon as possible. Practical steps might include:

– Reading through the Key Concepts and Processes of other arts subjects.

– Initiating a conversation with another arts teacher about their choice and use of technology for a particular piece of work.

– Using the Internet to broaden your own understanding of how other artists have begun to link together their own artistic practice with the work of other artists through new technologies.

To reiterate, a cross-curricular approach to teaching is characterised by sensitivity towards, and a synthesis of, knowledge, skills and understandings from various subject areas that inform an enriched pedagogy which promotes an approach to learning which embraces and explores this wider sensitivity through various methods. For us, within the arts, this starts with our own work as artists, musicians, designers, dancers and actors. From this solid starting point, we can begin to find cross-curricular links between our work through technology – our second key principle.

Principle 2: Technology builds bridges

For the majority of the arts subjects the role of the teacher is a vital one, not just for their pedagogical or instructional roles, but primarily for their role as a creative practitioner within the classroom. As we discussed above, finding these cross-curricular aspects within our work, and using technology to develop them, is a vital first step.

ICT can help build bridges between arts subjects in at least three ways: technologically, artistically and educationally. First, and technologically, there is an inherent potential with digital technologies to encourage cross-curricular work. After all, from the computer's perspective a piece of digital audio, film or photograph are, literally, a load of numbers! Therefore, it is not surprising that when we begin to look more closely at the pieces of technology that we could make use of in our teaching we find common ideas, metaphors and processes. A simple example of this would be the cut, copy and paste elements contained within the majority of most software's edit menu. Perhaps a little bit more elegantly, dig a little deeper into photo-editing software, digital video editors and digital audio sequencers and you will find common processing devices such as filters, granulation, inversion tools and other editing processes. All have a specific function within the software yet, at the same time, encourage a common approach to the constructing, editing and refinement of digital materials.

Second, in the wider artistic world, newer forms of technology have begun to transform what we might call traditional subject cultures in powerful ways. What might be summarised as an 'interdisciplinary' approach to the arts is obvious within each of our subject cultures. As we discussed in Chapter 4, many educators prefer the term 'interdisciplinary' to 'cross-curricular'. It has a particular resonance for us as artists. There are many examples of this that could be cited. Models of interdisciplinarity can be found in the film studio, with groups of different creative or artistic personnel such as set designers, foley artists, sound designers, composers, pre- and post-production editors, scriptwriters, and many more, employed in the pursuit of a common artistic goal. New forms of technology have been employed within what might be seen as relatively conservative art forms such as ballet, e.g. the TEEVE project saw ballet dancers using video-conferencing technologies to develop collaborative approaches to dance in an online environment (TEEVE 2010). Wherever one looks, artists collaborate and, in many cases, technology helps inform and develop these collaborations in interesting ways.

Third, and this is where we spend the majority of our time in this chapter, from an educational perspective there is an argument that technology can act as a bridge between subject cultures. This is particularly true within the arts. John's metaphor of 'trading zones' (John 2005: 471) helpfully examines what he calls the 'borderlands' between subjects and technology within which certain types of 'transactions' can take place. Using Galison's anthropological work as a starting point (Galison 1997), John explores the various subject subcultures within physics, analysing the various trading that takes place between theoreticians, experimentalists and engineers. He concludes:

> Exchanges between sub-cultures can be compared to the incomplete and partial relations which are established when different tribes come together for trading purposes. Each tribe can bring things to the 'trading space' and take things away; even sacred objects can be offered up and exchanged. This trading process also gives rise to new contact languages which are locally understood and co-ordinated.
>
> (John 2005: 485)

John suggests that the use of this 'trading zone' metaphor can help us understand more fully the transitory and evolving relationship between a subject culture and the technologies that are brought to bear upon it. The boundary between arts subjects and technology becomes permeable in such a model, with notions of success depending on the perceived value associated with the presented ideas, the way in which the participants act upon these and understand them. John is anticipating an evolutionary space, one in which the every element becomes interdependent:

'Transaction spaces' are evolutionary where the affordances and constraints of the situation, the tools, and the setting can facilitate further interaction as well as limit it. To occupy a 'trading zone' does not mean abandoning one's 'sacred' disciplinary 'home' nor allowing the 'profane' to dominate the exchange; rather it respects subtle negotiation and accommodation (Wertsch 2003; Claxton *et al.* 2003) processes that encourage multiple and modified identities to emerge over time.

(John 2005: 486)

Reflective task

This task explores how John's metaphor could be applied to your subject area, or collection of subject areas (e.g. the performing arts). Consider the following key questions drawn from his 'trading spaces' metaphor:

1. What are the key things that your subject area can bring to the space to 'trade' with others?

2. Are there any particularly sacred objects within your subject that you can bring with you? How would you feel about these objects being traded and used by others?

3. New types of conversations or collaborations (in John's terms, 'contact languages') could emerge through this process of trading. What characteristics might these new languages have? Will others be able to understand these or will they remain localised?

4. What would the relationship be between my 'sacred home' and these new collaborative, trading zones?

5. How can I ensure that any trading is conducted in a sensitive and empathetic manner, ensuring that the 'profane' does not dominate or exclude conversations with others?

As we considered in Chapter 4, playing creatively with metaphors is an essential skill in developing new approaches to working within and between our subjects. As arts educators, we believe that we should be leading the way on this type of activity. These questions may be challenging, but please use them to develop your own thinking and discuss them with colleagues from other subject areas too.

So, the argument here is that technological mediated exchanges or interactions of the type John is anticipating are something that all arts educators should aspire to develop in their work. This is a key way in which bridges can be built between our subjects. As we will see below, at their peak they may lead to opportunities for the emergence and establishment of new, cross-curricular artistic languages and pedagogies, locally situated and, perhaps, of value and understood only to those directly involved (but no less educationally valuable because of this). But this will only happen when the items or 'objects' that are being exchanged are of value. The reflective task asked you consider what the 'sacred objects' within your subject culture might be. Is there willingness on your part to offer these up within such an exchange and allow them to be negotiated with or compromised? Cross-curricular, collaborative approaches that dominate education today seem to be dominated by low value ('profane') exchanges. These are characterised by pieces of curriculum development that merge subjects down to their lowest common denominator, underplaying the well-established strengths of its subject culture and replacing these with hastily constructed and meaningless uses of technology which disempower teachers and cut short the opportunities for their students' learning. In contrast, high value exchanges will result in meaningful developments in arts education that centre on attributes that underpin ongoing teacher development. As John's conclusions assert:

> If this agenda is to materialise then schools and subjects need time to adjust to using ICT, to explore its possibilities and to engage with its affordances as well as understanding its constraints. Additionally, certain conditions need to be prevalent if the further blending of technology and pedagogy within subjects is to flourish. These conditions are dependent on a number of characteristics, all of which, according to Eraut (2001), are regarded as fundamental to the creation of a suitable organisational microclimate. They include:
> - A blame free culture;
> - Learning from experiences – positive and negative – at both group and individual levels;
> - Trying to make full use of the various knowledge resources held by members;
> - Encouraging talk about learning;
> - Locating and using relevant knowledge from outside the group;
> - Enhancing and extending understandings and capabilities of both the group as a whole and its individual members.
>
> (John 2005: 484–5)

This advice is timely. New ventures, of the type we are promoting throughout this book, will depend on a communal sense of enquiry that is dominated by characteristics such as those John identifies.

Principle 3: Technology that empowers and embraces

The first key principle for developing an approach to cross-curricular teaching and learning in the arts through technology focused on your work as a teacher and artist. The second principle discussed three ways in which technology can help build bridges between arts subjects (technologically, artistically and educationally). At the level of educational interactions between subjects, it built on a trading metaphor and suggested that cross-curricular trading processes between subjects could result in new artistic languages and, as we shall see below, pedagogies developing between teachers.

The third principle argues that technology has the ability to empower and embrace pupils from a broader spectrum than might have historically been engaged within arts subjects within the curriculum. Before we consider this statement in detail, the following case study will explore how technology has attracted one young person and provided them with the opportunity to work as a professional sound designer.

CASE STUDY 2: Painting in Sound

When I met Alex for the first time, he was working as a sound designer from his studio in the basement of his house in south Manchester under the shadow of Old Trafford, the Manchester United Football Club's stadium.[1] Interviewing Alex was a life-changing moment. Through his use of technology, he had not just opened the door, but blasted it off its hinges and learnt how to speak with a musical fluency and passion that was peculiarly infectious. Here was someone whose music education was the exact opposite of mine; no formal qualifications, no instrumental or conservatoire training; no 'advanced' (sic) level musical studies. Yet, his breadth of musical knowledge and experience put my own to shame; his compositional and improvisational abilities were outstanding; his ability to analyse, reflect on and communicate his musical intentions were breathtaking. What had facilitated these skills in him? What was his source of inspiration? The short answer was 'music':

> Music is - how can I describe it, it's so many things – it really has saved me from a life that – it's hard to explain. I grew up on an estate in Edinburgh and I used to get in quite a lot of trouble. Music saved me from a path that I could see leading to destruction and for that I'm very grateful. So I tend to treat music as a very good friend. It's something that's helped me to communicate with people, to express myself. It's a language that you can relate to people from different nations. It transcends limitations.
>
> (Alex, in interview, in Savage 2005b: 4)

It was interesting that Alex did not respond to this question with the answer, 'technology'. Technology, for Alex, was the tool, a powerful, facilitating tool that allowed him access to the world of music in a way that other tools had prevented.

At the time of my initial meetings with Alex, much of his musical language was, in John's terms, 'locally understood and co-ordinated' (John 2005: 486). However, in the intervening years, Alex has worked hard on his musical language and has become a leading, international sound designer. It has allowed him to transcend the limitations of his early educational and musical experiences. Now Alex stands on a par with professional composers and sound designers in a highly competitive commercial market. He speaks an articulate musical language that, importantly, is his own, authentic style (forged through the use of his technological tools).

Music was the key for Alex. But technology played its part too. As we will see below, ensuring that these two elements remain fused together in an appropriately balanced relationship will be key to ensuring that more young people become passionate about their own musical language.

So, to return to the statement at the beginning of this third principle, how can a cross-curricular approach to the use of technology in the arts empower and embrace a broader range of young people. We will use Alex and his work as an example; perhaps you can think of other people from your own subject specialism from whom similar lessons could be drawn?

First, technology does this because it provides an obvious link into the wider lives of the students that we teach. It taps into a whole range of skills, knowledge and understanding that young people today have grown up with in a way that many teachers did not. Alex's musical practice, as a performer and composer, were entirely dependent on his use of a range of music technologies. These technologies cover the analogue and digital range and include the latest and most powerful personal computers as well as vintage monophonic synthesisers and other pre-MIDI devices. Whilst one or two of these instruments had a piano-style keyboard, most did not bear any resemblance to what might be called a traditional musical instrument. The range of technology that Alex had at his disposal was matched by his sophisticated and flexible working practices within the studio environment. Alex was not, unlike many students in lessons in schools today, fixed in front of a computer screen. He is physically active within the studio, darting from place to place, animated and purposeful whilst tapping drum pads or setting patches, listening intently to mixes whilst experimenting in an improvisatory manner at his mixing desk. In interview, Alex expresses strongly the need for this kind of improvisatory play with technology:

> It is often the case that you'll get happy accidents. The way to get happy accidents is to throw things at each other and see if they work. And once you see that certain things do work you'll know that in the future you can have these two elements working together. Experiment, experiment, experiment and learn your craft. That's what it's all about.
>
> (Alex in interview, Savage 2005b: 5)

Second, technology engages young people through a language that they understand. This is an important point that builds on many of our arguments in Chapter 4. Alex, as an example, lacked a traditional musical vocabulary. He did not know what key his music was in, what chords it contained, nor could he compare the form of his compositions against any established, traditional models. Did this matter? Not to him. Rather, he had formed his own vocabulary about his creative practice as a sound designer, drawing on a whole array of terms from the visual arts, dance and contemporary film theory. His work presented an interesting, natural development of a cross-curricular use of language which was very empowering.

This interplay between the aural and visual domain, in particular how each could be used to reinforce the thinking, creative ideas, potential and understanding of the other was evidenced on many occasions. It also permeated through our conversations, where I was often struck by the strong visual metaphors he employed to describe his working practice:

> I feel that sound design is an area in which you can either paint with very large strokes or very fine strokes. You can go as deep as you like and put as much detail in as required. Or you can just paint with broad strokes.
>
> (Alex in interview, Savage 2005b: 7)

Waters, in a helpful exploration and extension of this theme, identifies a similar point:

> New technologies form a seductive meeting point for many previously separate arts practices. The generally uncritical acceptance of new tools, for example, the profusion of synthesisers in music classrooms, as a convenient means to the continuation of old concepts have tended to mask some of the more useful implications of the new technologies.
>
> (Waters 1994: 28)

Waters' criticism of how these tools have been used will be picked up below in our fourth and final principle. But, as we have already considered in our second principle, there will be a requirement for us as arts educators to facilitate a deeper cross-disciplinary interchange within this 'seductive meeting point' of new technologies. This will require us to consider how the language of our arts subjects might change and develop in light of the new approaches to technology that we are seeking to implement. If you were Alex's music teacher, would you be concerned about the fact that his whole compositional vocabulary was based around terminology drawn from the visual arts curriculum? Would it be enriching for him to extend this vocabulary into more musicology areas? This is not straightforward. Even a well-established composer of electro-acoustic music has aligned himself with art-forms outside of music itself:

> We have more in common with the filmmaker or the sculptor, the painter, with the plastic artist, than with the traditional musician. I really have that feeling, even though my origins are in traditional music.
>
> (Dhomont 2002)

John's anthropological approach to the establishment of new languages within trading zones (John 2005: 486) is an interesting metaphor through which one could analyse Alex's musical education. The language discourse of music technology is, in itself, highly metaphorical and makes connections across a range of trading zones. As we considered above, an analysis of language within a typical piece of sequencing software will uncover terminology such as cut, copy and paste (all of which are found within word processing and video editing software). But more widely, metaphorical links between music and art have a long history and have underpinned many cultural movements (Maur 1999). Alex's inquisitive mind had led him to make all kinds of interesting connections of this type. Many of these became inspirations for his compositional work. The key point was that this language developed naturally through Alex's use of technology in pursuit of an artistic end. Therein lies an important key for us as arts educators seeking to maximise the potential of technology as a tool for cross-curricular teaching and learning.

Before we move on to consider our fourth and final principle, a short detour will be made here to illustrate aspects of the three principles considered so far in a slightly different way.

Alex's work, described in Case Study 2, and John's metaphor (John 2005: 486) caused me to consider to what extent the artistic use of technology should be a distinct area of study. In our field of music education, students get the opportunity to study either 'music' or 'music technology'. Both areas are underpinned by identifiably discrete, yet artificial, sets of assumptions about the knowledge, skills and understanding that are important. Teachers talk about this issue in interesting ways. Case Study 3 takes up this point.

CASE STUDY 3: Technology's status within the arts

A recent piece of research for the Training and Development Agency (TDA) explored issues about technology and its use in music education. In interview, teachers were asked to comment on how they integrated music technology within their work. Here are two extracts:

Extract 1

Interviewer:	Tell me about your use of music technology in the department …
Teacher 1:	We have a range of technology for students who struggle to play a musical instrument. It is about providing them with an opportunity to play and compose music.
Interviewer:	What about those students who play a musical instrument?
Teacher 1:	Why would they want to use technology? They can play already.

Extract 2

Interviewer:	How do you decide who gets to study for a GCSE in Music?
Teacher 2:	The students can choose to do it.
Interviewer:	Is that it? Are there any conditions?
Teacher 2:	Not really. As long as they can play an instrument to a basic level I'm happy to let them do it.
Interviewer:	What do you mean by a 'basic level'?
Teacher 2:	About Grade 5 by the time they get to the end of Year 11. That's the standard the exam board sets.
Interviewer:	Really? What about music technology? Can they use that instead?
Teacher 2:	No, that's not really the same is it? They can use that as well but perhaps it is better covered in other courses we run.

(Both interviews were conducted by the author
as part of a research and development project
funded by the TDA and reported in Savage 2007).

Reflective task

Reflect on the following questions:

1. To what extent should students' work with technology be separate from other, related work within a subject discipline?

2. Are separate qualifications (e.g. for 'Music' and 'Music Technology', for 'Art' and 'Expressive Arts') really the way forward?

3. How does your subject differentiate between the 'technological' and 'non-technological' tools that students use within it? Are these distinctions helpful or unhelpful to your thinking, your pedagogy and your students' learning?

To our minds, these are artificial distinctions. Future approaches towards education within the arts need to place digital technologies firmly alongside other tools and approaches. There is no difference in an artistic sense. Having established this, the entirety of this book has argued that all arts subjects need to be placed more firmly within a cross-curricular approach to teaching and learning across the whole curriculum. This is not about watering down a subject culture through bland and mediocre curriculum collaborations. Rather, it is about individual teachers developing powerful, cross-curricular pedagogies that are outward looking, underpinned by a outward-looking perspective (see Chapter 7 in Savage 2011). It will see individual teachers wanting to maximise the opportunities for contextualising learning within a broader framework of teaching and learning, and responding positively to the new affordances of technological tools in a way that enhance, enrich and extend traditional approaches within their subject culture. This moves us on to our final, fourth principle for developing cross curricular approaches for teaching and learning in the arts through technology.

Principle 4: Technology and a transformative pedagogy

What are the implications of all of these ideas for your pedagogy as a teacher, and especially as a teacher of the arts? First, as you might expect by now, it does not mean that you have to reject everything that informs your pedagogy at the moment. Consider Théberge's view:

> Although there are certainly fundamental differences between electronic or digital technologies and acoustic instruments, such differences do not inevitably separate them from the broader continuum of musical expression; only the crudest technological determinism could support the argument that musicians approach these new technologies without bringing with them at least some of their own 'accumulated sensibilities' with regards to music making.
>
> (Théberge 1997: 159)

The same is true for a pedagogy that underpins the teaching of all arts subjects. Those 'accumulated sensibilities' of teaching the arts that have been established, tried and tested over the years are brought alongside newer approaches. Therefore, we do not need to replace what are the many positive teaching strategies and excellent curriculum content that are already in place. Rather, we need to build and develop authentic models of cross-curricular, ICT-mediated arts education inspired by and through the work of ICT 'experts' like Alex and others. Théberge's suggestion that a piece of technology is, in a sense, created or recreated by the user in the act of making is relevant to us as teachers and our students as learners. We are all 'consumers of technology' and our 'ability to define, at least partially, the meaning and use of the technology is an essential assumption and theoretical point of departure' for any truly creative work (Théberge 1997: 160).

Part of this wider definition of technological use is the context of teaching and pedagogy within which these technologies will be used. So, second, it is fair to assume that whilst core elements of our subject cultures will remain in place, there will be room for new, cross-curricular pedagogies inspired and infiltrated by the technologies we choose to use within our teaching. We should expect pupils to learn about our subject with technologies in ways that are different from our existing practices. But we should not throw the baby out with the proverbial bath water. It is not that traditional concepts, forms and processes have had their day. Rather, it is a reprioritising and reordering of what is important at any one given moment in that particular educational context that matters. The empowering features of a broad, cross-curricular disposition within this process are substantial.

These two points can be brought into focus through considering a specific aspect of every teacher's pedagogy – the use of learning objectives. In Chapter 2 of this book we considered how knowledge and learning could be organised within a cross-curricular approach. Part of this involved us reflecting on the difference between 'learning' and 'doing'. We made the point that it is often easy to get the two confused. Separating the 'learning' from the 'doing' is an important element in writing a well-formed learning objective. The clear identification and definition of what the pupils will learn by the teacher, in advance of a lesson, is now seen as a vital, unquestionable and integral part of their preparation. However, for many teachers of the arts this has always been problematic. At a basic level, prescribing the outcomes of an artistic activity takes away its sense of discovery and creation. Pupils, in our experience, quickly realise that their supposedly artistic activities follow a predetermined pathway and seek to conform appropriately. Alternatively,

> In the arts and in subject matters where, for example, novel or creative responses are desired, the particular behaviours to be developed cannot easily be identified. Here curriculum and instruction should yield behaviours or products which are unpredictable. The end achieved ought to be something of a surprise to both teacher and pupil.
>
> (Eisner 1985: 33)

One might ask how often we feel this element of surprise that Eisner suggests should be accompanying the processes and products of truly creative work in the classroom. In observations of Alex's improvisatory approach to sound design, it is clear that his work with new technologies is not easily predictive or defined through simple learning statements. In many cases his musical expression was nurtured and developed through a process of germinating and experimenting with ideas, trial and error, choosing from multiple compositional possibilities and pathways and constantly searching for appropriate, responsive structural devices. None of these are easy to prescribe in advance. But Eisner's notion of expressive outcomes rather than expressive objectives seems eminently sensible and maps out a potential way forward. Expressive outcomes are 'the outcomes that students realise in the course of a curriculum activity, whether or not they are the particular outcomes sought' (Eisner 2002: 161). At a basic level this type of objective relates neatly with Alex's conjecture to 'Experiment, experiment, experiment!'

Developing cross-curricular approaches to the arts through technology is about harnessing the powerful force of new technology within a pedagogy that maintains a firm grip on the broader aesthetic preoccupations of one's particular subject. It is about a balance between remaining true and faithful to the key concepts and process that really underpin one's subject whilst, simultaneously, recognising that subjects themselves are being transformed by new approaches many of which are inspired by the potential of new technologies to blur subject boundaries. Pedagogy has an important part of play in this. Pedagogy is both a 'practice' and a 'process' (Bernstein 1999: 259; Popkewitz 1998: 536) through which certain things can be acquired or through which certain capabilities can be developed. In the accompanying title to this book (Savage 2011), an argument was made that skilful teachers embody a skilful pedagogy. This skilful pedagogy has to be developed at some point. The ideas and practices of developing a pedagogical approach to cross-curricular teaching and learning, inspired by technology within the arts may well, in Bruner's terms, 'compete with, replace, or otherwise modify' your current pedagogical thinking and practice (Bruner 1996: 46).

One of the greatest advocates for pedagogy in recent times has been Professor Robin Alexander, a Fellow of Wolfson College at the University of Cambridge, and Director of the Cambridge Primary Review. His view is that 'it is schooling that has reduced knowledge to 'subjects' and teaching to mere telling' (Alexander 2008: 141). As teachers within creative subjects, it is time for us to rediscover a pedagogy for teaching the arts that transcends subjects and mere telling. Technology can play a role in this. But your involvement as a teacher is crucial. Research done at the University of Bristol pointed to

> … the importance of the teacher and the ways in which technology is incorporated into their pedagogy. This emphasises the importance of the ecological setting of classrooms and how a mixture of teachers' subject and pedagogical understandings act as filters during planning, practice and reflection.
>
> (Sutherland and John 2005: 411)

The role of the teacher was fundamental in incorporating technology within the classroom. One of the key future challenges facing educational communities will be the creation of opportunities for teachers to debate and discuss the educational purposes for, and philosophy underpinning, new technological approaches to teaching and learning. Teachers need to have a meaningful say in this ongoing debate, challenging and critiquing ideas so that the future shape of curriculum initiatives have a greater degree of shared ownership and, it is hoped, a wider impact. Facer calls this a 'curriculum for networked learning' and defines it as '… enabling individuals to learn to work effectively within social networks for educational, social and civic purposes and to develop strategies to establish and mobilise social networks for their own purposes' (Facer 2009: 7).

For teachers and learners the degree of personalisation within such a network is significant and should allow for the development of powerful processes for the development of subject knowledge and curriculum development. It will also facilitate the cross-subject exchanges or transactions that we have been discussing above. From the perspective of the learner (and this would include teachers as well as students), such a curriculum might consist of opportunities for:

- Learning and working within meaningful socio-technical networks not wholly within single educational institutions.
- Being assessed in interaction with tools, resources and collaborators.
- Developing capacities to manage information and intellectual property, building reputation and trust, developing experience of working remotely and in mediated environments.
- Creating new, personalised learning networks.
- Reflecting upon how learning is connected with other areas of personal, social, and working lives and manage and negotiate these relationships.
- Exploring the human-machine relationships involved in socio-technical networks.

(Facer 2009: 7)

The days of the individual teacher, teaching their individual subject in their own classroom, with the door closed to the majority of others outside, are clearly numbered. Key technological developments have already facilitated a significant shift in individual subject cultures, curriculum design and delivery. The role of technology within teaching and learning is powerful. Allying technology to the promotion of a cross-curricular approach to teaching and learning makes sense in many ways, not least in the educational benefits that it brings to students and teachers and the way that it reflects the wider use of technology outside the world of education. Networking and collaborative approaches are a key way forward.

Practical task

This task will involve you working with at least one other colleague from a different arts subject area from your own.

Working with your colleague(s), discuss the following questions:

- What are the elements of your subject culture that facilitate or constrain the adoption of technological tools within it?
- Having read through these four principles, what are your thoughts about a possible, probable or preferred model of cross-curricular arts education with technology in the future?

Identify a sequence of lessons that you are both going to teach at some point in the near future to the same group of pupils (e.g. a particular form group). Focus on one of the four principles that we have discussed above:

1. *Technology and your artistic practice*

2. *Technology builds bridges*

3. *Technology that empowers and embraces*

4. *Technology and a transformative pedagogy*

Work together on developing an approach to your teaching in these lessons that explores the chosen principle in a significant way. Start from your own subject perspective. Describe to your colleague(s) what you might do. Try to use each others' responses to inform your own approach. Revise these.

Teach through the series of lessons. Do not tell the pupils that you are doing anything different. After each lesson is complete, make a few notes about your thoughts or reflections on the lesson and how the principle you are exploring affected your choices as a teacher, the activities the pupils completed and the learning they engaged with.

Meet up with your colleague(s) again. Share your experiences and evaluate your work together.

Conclusion

It is always wise to look ahead, but difficult to look further than you can see.

This quotation from Winston Churchill is apposite for a chapter that deals with technology and its potential to facilitate cross-curricular approaches to teaching and learning. As we have pointed out, in many educational contexts around the world the use of ICT has increased rapidly. There have been significant pieces of research related to curriculum design, teacher pedagogy and ways of learning with technology. Many of these have impacted on the work of arts educators in positive ways. But this is not a time for self-congratulation or passive reflection. Outside the often-closeted world of education, technological developments continue to move forwards rapidly. Hardly a week goes by without comment in the international press about a new technological innovation or application related to the production, reception or consumption of art in one form or another. Over the last year or so, issues such as the establishment of an agency for navigating online copyright issues for film have been discussed (Fitzsimmons 2009), new systems to help train people to use prosthetic limbs using Guitar Hero (a music video game) have been developed (Graham 2009), and iPhone and iPod Touch owners have seen the development of a plethora of applications to create original artworks, play virtual pianos, drums and guitars and much more besides (Apple 2009). As we write this book, the launch of the new Apple iPad is already generating ideas about potential artistic applications before it has reached widespread uptake (Frankel 2010). As developments in technology move relentlessly forwards, there are the twin dangers facing educators: moving too quickly or too slowly. Either way, disjunctions between the pedagogy and practice of arts education have been noted, in school-based education (Savage 2004: 167; Cain 2004: 217; Ofsted 2009b: 34) and higher education (Draper 2008: 137; Jenkins *et al.* 2007: 129). Now, more than ever, arts educators need to be maintain their focus on what constitutes effective teaching and learning with technology. In other words:

> Change is now a constant condition in our education system, reflecting changes in the wider world. This has implications for teacher identity and role. What sort of teacher development is needed in order to keep pace with such change? We have to ask ourselves whether we want a mere 'retooling' of teacher competencies for specific purposes, or an approach that supports a renaissance in teacher development for an uncertain future. This is not about making an industrial process more efficient; rather, it is about enabling cultural change in the profession.
>
> (Futurelab 2006, p.39)

What will the future of arts education look like? How will the use of technology shape and mediate the cross-curricular educational processes that underpin it? It would be a bold writer who would predict, with any certainty, the changes and technological developments that our educational futures will contain. This chapter has not focused on this type of guesswork (educated or otherwise). The Futurelab report quoted above argues for a change in approach for teachers' professional development with technology. It acknowledges that the processes by which teachers learn about new technologies are complicated and constricted in various ways. But:

> The possibilities for real change in the system do exist. If we can bring the technologies into situations *that resonate strongly with teachers' sense of professional and moral purposes*, we may yet see what might truly prove to be a renaissance, in which teachers would employ digital technologies for 'understanding, reflection, ingenuity and creativity', and, through these, support their own learning in new ways.
>
> (Futurelab 2006: 41 [emphasis added])

As we have discussed above, the best chances of technology having a positive educational impact lie with teachers aligning these powerful tools to their own sense of professional purpose. An essential part of this professional purpose lies within the notion of subject cultures. Within the arts, as we have seen, these play a vital role in shaping our philosophy and practice about why the arts are important, how they should be represented and taught within our schools.

There will be no cross-curricular technological developments in arts education without teacher development. The fact that you have bought this book and read this far indicates to us that you want, hopefully, to engage with the transformations that are required to teach in a cross-curricular way with new technologies. These issues are more widely connected to other important, informing aspects of your work as a teacher. This chapter is part of a broader narrative about the positioning of arts subjects within the curriculum and the potential benefits to the arts, and other subjects, of teachers becoming more cross-curricular in their thinking and pedagogy. We will be returning to some of these themes in Chapter 7, where we examine what the future directions of teaching and learning in secondary education within the arts may be leading.

Professional Standards for QTS

This chapter will help you meet the following Q standards: Q16, 17, 23, 25a.

Professional Standards for Teachers

This chapter will help you meet the following core standards: C17, C27, C29a, C40, C41.

Notes

1 The Old Trafford ground is, rather appropriately to this context, often referred to as the 'theatre of dreams'.

Artistic approaches to assessment

Key objectives

By the end of this chapter, you will have:

- Thought about uses and purposes of assessment
- Considered how assessment can be utilised in cross-curricular teaching and learning
- Thought about planning for the effective use of formative assessment in your teaching

Introduction

Assessment is a key issue in contemporary educational discourse. It is, rightly, of concern to pupils, teachers, senior leadership teams, Ofsted, parents and carers, the media, local and national government. But, even with all this attention, sadly what this does not mean is that teachers have a wealth of materials upon which to draw, or expertise in assessment involving the arts upon which to call. Indeed, there are significant issues in the arts with regard to assessment, with a whole spectrum of opinions as to the utility (or otherwise) of assessment in the classroom.

> ### Reflective task
>
> What do you think of when 'assessment' is mentioned?
>
> What do your own assessment arrangements entail?
>
> Are you under any pressure with regards to assessment? If so, what/how?
>
> Are you satisfied with your current assessment arrangements?

There will be many answers to these questions, and it will be interesting to see if your views change as a result of reading this chapter. In order to begin to think in more detail about assessment, the first thing we need to do is clarify the assessment terminologies we shall be using, as these have tended to mutate somewhat, and can mean different things in different places.

Clarifying terminologies

The first area of assessment terminology that needs to be established is the differences between formative and summative assessment. These terms are well known and well used in education, so should be familiar. Summative assessment is assessment which occurs at specific points in the education of a student, and is used to summarise, or sum-up attainment.

> in the case of summative assessment there are various ways in which the information about student achievement at a certain time is used. These uses include: internal school tracking of students' progress; informing parents, students and the students' next teacher of what has been achieved; certification or accreditation of learning by an external body; and selection for employment or higher education.
>
> (Harlen 2005: 208)

Summative assessments can also become 'high-stakes' if they occupy a major certification role, for example GCSE or A-level.

A useful set of definitions of summative assessment is provided by Harlen and James:

- It takes place at certain intervals when achievement has to be reported.
- It relates to progression in learning against public criteria.
- The results for different pupils may be combined for various purposes because they are based on the same criteria.
- It requires methods which are as reliable as possible without endangering validity.
- It requires some quality assurance procedures.
- It should be based on evidence from the full range of performance relevant to the criteria being used.

> (Harlen and James 1997: 373)

Formative assessment is also referred to as assessment for learning (AfL). Although there are some who say there are differences between the two, we use the terms interchangeably throughout this book. Unlike summative assessment, formative assessment is concerned with working *with* the learners in order to improve the next stages of their learning. In other words:

> Formative assessment is that process of appraising, judging or evaluating students' work or performance and using this to shape and improve their competence. In everyday classroom terms this means teachers using their judgements of children's knowledge or understanding to feed back into the teaching process and to determine

for individual children whether to re-explain the task/concept, to give further practise on it, or move on the next stage.

(Tunstall and Gipps 1996: 389)

What this means is that formative assessment involves a dynamic interaction; this can be between teacher and pupil, or between pupils. In the case of ipsative assessment it involves the learner's own metacognitive processes. If the interaction involves the teacher, then one of the important outcomes should be that the teacher then takes some sort of appropriate action based on what they have found out as a result of the formative assessment process. In other words:

in order to serve a formative function, an assessment must yield evidence that, with appropriate construct-referenced interpretations, indicates the existence of a gap between actual and desired levels of performance, and suggests actions that are in fact successful in closing the gap

(Wiliam and Black 1996: 543)

Wiliam and Black are quite explicit here that formative assessment needs to have a role which 'suggests actions' that can be taken. This can involve the teacher re-engineering aspects of the learning programme, or it might involve the learner(s) being given appropriately differentiated materials in order to help them take the next steps themselves. It is sometimes observed that summative assessment is *done to* the learners, whereas formative assessment is *done with* them. Figure 6.1 gives a diagrammatic representation of these differing assessment modalities.

Alongside formative and summative assessment, Figure 6.1 also shows *the formative use of summative assessment*. This is an important distinction to be drawn, and is central to our clarification of terminologies. We have seen how formative assessment involves a dynamic interaction, and how summative assessment occurs at fixed points in the teaching and learning cycle. What has happened in many schools is that teachers have

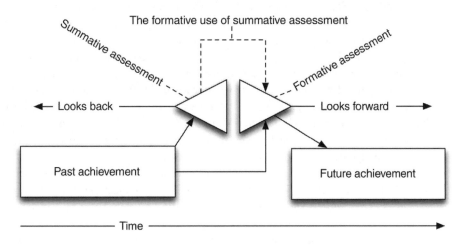

Figure 6.1 Assessment modalities (source: Fautley and Savage 2008: 27).

reconceived their assessment practices so that their regular and ongoing assessment practices have become based on summative assessments, which they then use to give formative feedback:

> because formative assessment has to be carried out by teachers, there is an assumption that all assessment by teachers is formative, adding to the blurring of the distinction between formative and summative purposes and to teachers changing their own on-going assessment into a series of 'mini' assessments each of which is essentially summative in character
>
> (Harlen and James 1997: 365)

This is an important distinction to make. Using summative assessments in a formative fashion is not of itself problematic, indeed, there can be many occasions when it is an appropriate thing to do. Where it does become an issue is where such assessments, and the concomitant grades which are awarded, are assumed to be true formative assessment. As Gordon Stobart observes:

> Such grading often masks a confusion, as it is described as formative (since it informs about progress and standards reached) when the function is really summative (a snapshot of where I am now)
>
> (Stobart 2008: 159)

Teachers of the arts have traditionally been used to incorporating formative assessment into teaching and learning in their classes, and were probably doing so long before the terminology came into everyday usage. Indeed, it is hard to imagine teaching and learning situations in the arts where there is not some form of interaction between the teacher and learners with regard to ways in which the pupils might develop their own learning, and take it forwards to the next stage. This is so well built-in to teaching and learning in the arts that it was a music lesson that was chosen in the early days of the government-sponsored Key Stage 3 strategy materials for teachers to show formative assessment (DfES 2002). This way of working came as something of a shock to teachers of subjects other than the arts, as this non-arts teacher commented, '… do you mean I have to have conversations with my pupils, I'm not used to doing that in my subject' (Fautley 2007: 3). What has happened since is that well-meaning arts teachers, under pressure from school assessment managers, themselves not normally from an arts background, have told arts teachers that they are doing formative assessment 'wrongly', and need to change their practices. This has led to a certain amount of 'terminology slip' in terms of what is meant by assessment which is *formative*, and so it is important to clarify at the outset what we are talking about.

Another area where problems can arise is when assessment data designed for one use is then put to an entirely different use altogether. For example, suppose a group of teachers have designed an assessment task for the half-way stage of a piece of cross-curricular teaching and learning, and which involves the pupils working together in order to solve a problem of some sort. The reasons the teachers have designed this task include the following:

- To see how well the pupils are working co-operatively.

- To find out what information they have gained from the first part of the teaching and learning programme.

- To see what emphases are needed in the next part of the teaching and learning programme.

- To see if pupils in different classes are achieving in different areas.

- … and probably many more besides!

The information this assessment task yields, known as assessment data, is meant to help the teacher and the pupils. If it is then passed on to the school's assessment manager it could be put to all sorts of purposes for which it was not intended, including comparing attainment in the arts with other subjects (remember, this was an interim assessment during a programme of teaching and learning), comparing the attainment of pupils with different teachers, comparing attainment between different schools, and so on. The results of this is that assessment data designed for one use is being treated as unproblematic when being put to other uses. David Boud refers to this as assessments having to do 'double duty', in that:

> • They have to encompass formative assessment for learning and summative for certification
> • They have to have a focus on the immediate task and on implications for equipping students for … [the] future
>
> (Boud 2000: 160)

This double duty of assessment is something teachers of the arts might want to be aware – and wary – of. Whist we do not want to overburden ourselves or our students with assessments, we do want them to be fit for purpose, and not misused for purposes for which they were never intended.

For whom is the assessment intended?

This takes us to an important question with regards to assessment in cross-curricular teaching and learning, this is for whom is the assessment intended? In simplistic terms, there are three possible audiences for assessments, these are the teacher, the pupils and systemic purposes, in other words, the sorts of users we discussed with regards to assessment doing double duty above. This is an important topic to think about, because the audience for the assessment to some degree drives the type of assessment which is undertaken. Figure 6.2 gives a diagrammatic representation of this:

Figure 6.2 shows quite clearly that there is a complex interrelationship between the uses to which assessment data can be put. From the perspective of the teacher it is appropriate to think about these uses at the time of designing assessments. After all giving an assessment which shows the teacher how well the pupils have learned aspects of a particular topic (and concomitantly how well the teacher has taught it), might not be appropriate for systemic utilisation with regard to assumptions concerning measures of

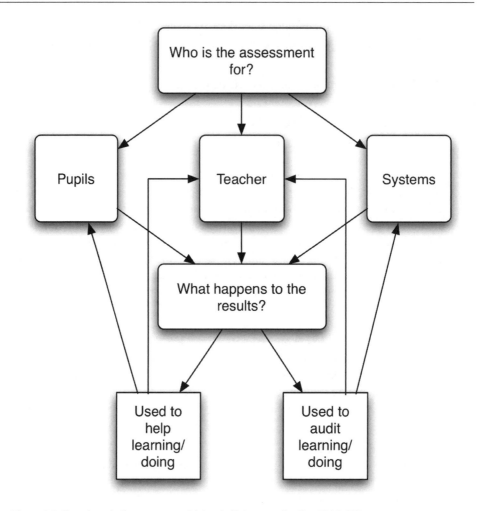

Figure 6.2 For whom is the assessment intended? (source: Fautley 2010: 70).

pupil attainment. The reason for considering this with relation to cross-curricular teaching and learning is that it is important to keep in mind that the sorts of assessments we shall be discussing in this chapter are mostly those which can be used directly to help improve learning. We shall be concerned to some extent with auditing learning too, but our main concern will be with those assessments which are directly of help to the teacher and the pupils in the classroom.

Cross-curricular teaching and learning and extant assessment

One of the problems which will be faced early on in the design of assessments in cross-curricular teaching and learning programmes is likely to be that of fitting with current assessment arrangements, This is particularly significant at Key Stage 3, where the National Curriculum requires subject-specific assessment to be undertaken.

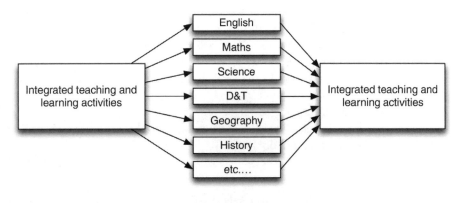

Separated assessments

Figure 6.3 Subject-specific assessment.

Figure 6.3 shows the problematic pathway which single subject based assessment has when it occurs in integrated cross-curricular teaching and learning activities. This is because of the interplay of the issues first explored with relation to Figure 6.2. The dominance of an external assessment regime in the form of National Curriculum levels means that for many teachers, one of the main problems with cross-curricular teaching and learning, is how to relate the new ways of working that this espouses with existing subject-based assessment criteria. In many cases we know that one of the effects of this is to downplay the assessments which the teachers themselves actually undertake, their own teacher assessment (TA). As Hall and Harding note with regard to TA:

> It is not surprising that the high stakes nature of this assessment agenda, with its published performance tables, its target setting based on national test results, its assumption that standards can be objectively measured ... that TA, which is dependent on teacher judgement, is not prioritized.
>
> (Hall and Harding 2002: 12)

What many teachers can end up doing under these circumstances is to conceptualise *all* of the assessments which they undertake from within a framework of National Curriculum levels, despite the recommendation from the then QCA that 'a single piece of work will not cover all the expectations set out in a level description' and that National Curriculum levels were originally designed for use only at the end of the Key Stage. Teachers who have had to work within these paradigms found it initially problematic, as this drama teacher working on a cross-curricular teaching and learning programme observed:

> their [the student's] knowledge is really still difficult for us to measure I think, we still haven't quite got our heads around each other's subject areas. So I really, really struggled to assess my science last enterprise, and was way too high in my marks, and the class that I just got their drama marks are very, very high, and I wouldn't be giving them marks like that, and that's a test of ... using national curriculum levels, they have

the levels. ... so what am I doing, RE, history, geography, drama, science, I'm levelling mine in, and on each report at the end of term I level them in each of those things according to the national curriculum level ... I think that where we've struggled with that is not knowing each other's levels or the expectations of the kids enough. ... I think there's a lot of score in the levels in that you have a dialogue then, as soon as you're talking about 'right you're level 2' or 'you're level 3 what's your target' and I think those are important to target setting, and you and the kids have a shared understanding of what a level 3 is, and without a level descriptor you haven't got that, so I think it's important to do that

(Fautley *et al.* 2008: 80–1)

One of the reasons for this drama teacher's concerns was that she was having to provide National Curriculum levels in subjects in which she did not feel she had insider knowledge. For those teachers who have to do this on a regular basis in their cross-curricular teaching and learning work, there seems to have emerged a set of similar strategies which are employed to deal with this issue. What this often entails is the production of an *assessment matrix* which maps attainment in the various National Curriculum subject areas covered by the cross-curricular teaching and learning programme, and accompany this with assessment criteria statements. The assessment criteria statements delineate in some detail the expected attainment from students specific to the cross-curricular teaching and learning programme in question. This solves the issue of giving single subject-based National Curriculum criteria from within a cross-curricular teaching and learning programme. Operationalisation of this methodology is evidenced in the comments of this teacher:

[Assessment] has been formalised ... one of the massive advances is the work that [the course co-ordinator] has done in terms of paring down all of the National Curriculum's assessment guidance into one very concise set of instructions about the meaning of level 3, level 4, level 5, level 6 and so on and the creation of this generic, very concise model of levelling that we can all use.

(Fautley *et al.* 2008: 81)

However, we need to be clear: what an assessment matrix of this sort tends to be doing is fulfilling the need for what we referred to in Figure 6.2 as a systems requirement for assessment data. Whilst in many schools students and parents want to know what level they are, this in itself will not help students' learning to improve.

Learning outcomes

In the overarching book which accompanies this one, it is noted that:

there will be learning objectives and outcomes that touch on ... other subjects implicated through the lesson activities, choice of resources and associated learning outcomes.

(Savage 2011: 149)

The point to pick up here is the notion of 'learning objectives and outcomes'. There are a number of ways of describing these, and it may be that in your school you use a different phrase. The important thing is that these are statements about what learning will take place in a lesson. But in a cross-curricular teaching and learning programme it is likely to be the case there will be a wider variety of learning than the traditional delivery mode of single subject lessons, and that this learning could take place in a variety of ways and sequences.

Reflective task

How might the non-linear nature of cross-curricular teaching and learning programmes in the arts affect the writing of learning outcome statements?

This issue can be one of the hardest things for teachers to 'let go' of in the transition to cross-curricular teaching and learning programmes. Writing learning outcomes has become a standard part of pedagogic activity. Indeed, viewed from a reductionist standpoint it can become a case of 'tell the students what they are going to learn – teach it to them – tell them what they have learned'. Reduced to this (admittedly) over-simplified form then school days must become a bit of a chore for learners. Ofsted have observed that 'in the best provision, teachers were aware of the need to "do more of less"' (Ofsted 2009b: 14). One of the ways that this can be done is to think about longer teaching and learning programmes.

The sorts of cross-curricular teaching and learning programmes we have been discussing in this book, indeed throughout this series of books, are not necessarily amenable to the atomistic deconstruction of sequential learning strategies. Does this matter? It does if you have to write three learning outcomes on the board at the start of the lesson! But in some of the cross-curricular teaching and learning programmes we have been discussing, it may well be inappropriate to tell the students in advance precisely *what* they will be learning, as guided discovery learning can be a powerful tool.

The role of formative assessment

> When teachers evaluate there is a tendency to conflate attention to a student's product with the desire to record the student's learning.
>
> (Sefton-Green 2000: 217)

We have touched on aspects of the process-product dichotomy before in this book; in the matter of assessment this becomes a key distinction to be drawn. Julian Sefton-Green draws our attention to the danger of conflating attention to the product with an evaluation of the learning that has preceded its production. It is in the ongoing day-to-day formative assessment conversations that you have with your students where you form judgements, discuss with them, and help the students with their work, that will make the most difference. Doing this you are assessing the processes of learning which the students are undertaking. You are deciding whether or not to intervene, and, if you decide that you will, you are deciding what form that intervention should take. You are thinking about what you will say to the pupils, considering their answers to your questions, teasing out from them their potential understandings, and making on-the-hoof decisions about what the most efficacious thing to say and/or do next might be. All of these are formative assessment strategies. We saw above how teachers of the arts' traditional strengths in formative assessment have been eroded by assessment managers, but in the key area of making a difference in the classroom, these conversations you are having, where the ebb and flow of talk leads to developments in the students' learning, are fundamental to formative assessment. You may not be giving them a level or a grade, marking their work, or recording anything in your mark-book, but you are doing formative assessment. Indeed, as Dylan Wiliam, one of the gurus of formative assessment, said:

> If what you are doing under the heading of assessment for learning involves putting anything into a spreadsheet, then you are not doing the assessment for learning that makes the most difference to student learning
>
> (SSAT website n.d.)

The key aspect of what you are doing, however, is *feedback*, and it is worth spending a little time thinking about the role of feedback in cross-curricular teaching and learning programmes in the arts.

The role of feedback

The notion of feedback is an important one in formative assessment. As we have seen, it involves a dialogue between teacher and pupils concerning what the pupils are doing at present, and what they need to do next. As the Assessment Reform Group (ARG) put it:

> Learners need information and guidance in order to plan the next steps in their learning. Teachers should: pinpoint the learner's strengths and advise on how to develop them; be clear and constructive about any weaknesses and how they might be addressed; provide opportunities for learners to improve upon their work
>
> (Assessment Reform Group 2002: 2)

This asks quite a lot of you as a teacher. Indeed, to undertake formative assessment well is challenging:

> formative assessment is a central part of pedagogy. This explains why many teachers find it hard to implement; it may challenge them to change what they do, how they think about learning and teaching, and the way in which they relate to their pupils.
>
> (Mansell *et al.* 2009: 9)

This is because as a result of being involved in feedback you will be thinking about the ways in which you organise teaching and learning in your classroom; indeed, you will be doing more than thinking, you will be enacting change, and responding to the needs of your learners. It is for this reason that feedback is sometimes referred to as *feedforward*, as it being used to make a difference to learning which has not yet taken place.

Assessment criteria

In Chapter 3, especially in Figure 3.2, we looked at the non-linear routes students can take through cross-curricular teaching and learning programmes involving the arts. What the teachers who have been planning the programme, represented by the non-linear route on the left hand side of the figure, are likely to have produced is what we referred to before as an assessment matrix. This will involve a series of assessment criteria statements. Assessment criteria themselves are quite difficult to write, and we know that a common issue is that teachers take the National Curriculum level statements for individual subjects, and try to disassemble them into specific competencies, often behaviouristic in nature. One of the issues with writing assessment criteria is to have regard for what is being assessed, and the reasons for it.

Reflective task

Have you written assessment criteria in the past at all?

Who were they for?

What did you do with them?

What was their purpose?

We discussed the notion of learning outcomes above, and a well-written learning outcome can become its own assessment criterion. If you have written assessment criteria in the past separate from learning outcomes, you may have found it to be quite problematic. There are a number of factors to be taken into account when devising assessment criteria, and in our case, devising assessment criteria for cross-curricular teaching and learning involving the arts, one very important decision needs to be tackled at the outset. This is:

■ Do I try to tie my assessment criteria to National Curriculum levels, or not?

The importance of this question cannot be overemphasised. But answering it requires a whole series of other factors to be taken into account! These include:

■ Am I writing these criteria to help the pupils, or …

■ Am I writing them to provide data for 'the system'?

■ Do I want to show comparability with other subjects?

■ Does my school insist all assessments involve (subdivided?) National Curriculum levels?

■ Do I want to baseline assess the students? In other words …

- Do I want to show that cross-curricular learning is at least as efficacious as single-subject learning?
- Do I want the results from this assessment to be made public?
- How will this assessment be done? Task – Test – Teacher Assessment – Pupil (self/peer) assessment?
- … and many more besides!

These are questions that will be specific to each context. It is impossible to provide general answers, as every school's requirements will be different. But what can be thought about are some of the reasons for tying assessment criteria to National Curriculum levels. In many cases the prime reason for doing this seems to be that level statements have become ubiquitous, and there are no other assessment tools available. Indeed, there are stories of Ofsted inspectors stopping students in corridors and asking them what level they are in specific subjects. This has led to a climate where it seems that everything has to be given a National Curriculum level, and an assessment cannot be regarded as such unless it results in a level. But this does not need to be always the case. If the answer to the first question in the list above is 'Yes, I am writing these to help the pupils', then a level statement may not be the best way of doing this.

We discuss skills, and skill acquisition a number of times during the course of this book. It is quite likely that during the course of a cross-curricular teaching and learning programme some sort of skill acquisition or development will take place. These could be artform specific skills, PLTS, social and emotional skills, literacy, numeracy or other non-arts skills. What many teachers find helpful is to have a taxonomy of skills that they wish to assess. Writing criteria statements for skill acquisition is fine, but we do need to be aware of some of the issues assessment of skill acquisition can bring. Chief amongst these is to assume that to assess skills is to assess the entirety of learning! We have already seen in previous chapters that understanding is a key teaching and learning objective. It is possible to reproduce skills without understanding, so mistaking one for the other needs to be avoided.

Criteria for criteria

So, whether dealing with skills, concepts, constructs, or understanding, when writing assessment criteria here are some of the issues that need to be borne in mind:

Criteria for criteria:

- A criterion should be assessable in some way.
  - ☐ It should be possible to ascribe a differentiated value to the criterion.
- A criterion should have some relationship to the whole.
  - ☐ It should not be evaluating an irrelevant or tangential aspect of accomplishment.
- A criterion should be isolatable as much as possible.
  - ☐ If you are assessing, say, process of a creative activity, this might not be relate to assessment of the product.
- Just because something is easy to assess does not mean it is worth assessing!
  - ☐ This is where easily assessable skill acquisition can be mistaken for assessment of understanding of the construct. And, conversely …

- Just because something is hard to assess does not mean it should be ignored.
  - ☐ If you are looking, for example, for a quality performance, this is a hard thing to write a criterion for, but as it might be what the whole cross-curricular teaching and learning programme is aiming towards, omitting it seems odd!

These 'criteria for criteria' will need contextualising within the circumstances within which they are being employed. They can be used in a summative fashion at the end of a teaching and learning programme, or aspects of them can be used formatively as the teaching and learning progresses.

We have deliberately not tried to tie these in to National Curriculum levels. What our main concern has been here is to think about the ways in which assessment can be used to take the learning of students forwards, in other words to provide helpful formative assessments, and summative assessments which can be used in formative fashion. To help with this process, let us deconstruct the criteria within the context of cross-curricular teaching and learning programmes which involve the arts.

A criterion should be assessable in some way

One of the purposes of summative assessment is to ascribe a value to something; the purpose of formative assessment is to help the learner. But it is important not to assume these are different types of assessment:

> It is sometimes difficult to avoid referring to these as if they were different forms or types of assessment. They are not. They are discussed separately only because they have different purposes; indeed the same information, gathered in the same way, would be called formative if it were used to help learning and teaching, or summative if it were not so utilized but only employed for recording and reporting. While there is a single clear use if assessment is to serve a formative purpose, in the case of summative assessment there are various ways in which the information about student achievement at a certain time is used.
>
> (Harlen 2005: 208)

What this means is that the teacher needs to be clear about what is done with the assessment data that that is produced. In the case of a criterion being assessable in a differentiated fashion, one of the simplest forms is to use a three point scale, corresponding to - / = / +. Or, to use the old National Curriculum terminology with which many teachers are familiar, working towards/working at/working beyond. These can also be written as: not yet able to (or, in ZPD fashion, able to with assistance)/able to/able to well. The exact wording can be altered to meet the specific wants and needs of the circumstance. As we are reminded in the accompanying book (Savage, 2010: 147), manageability of assessment data is a key issue for teachers. This simple scale has manageability in its favour. It is, of course, but one among many differentiated grading systems, we are merely pointing out that to write an assessment criterion does need to take into account some form of differentiation in terms of the grading method which should be integral to it, and any suitable grading method can be applied, but the important thing is that a differentiated grade can be applied to it.

When used in a formative fashion, employment of the grade alone may not always be sufficient. Saying to a student 'you are working towards level 4b, but have not achieved it yet', or, 'you get a level 3c for this', does not tell the learner what to do to improve. For this the learner needs to be helped *specifically* to know what to do next, in terms of attainable target setting.

Classroom story

In one school the students all have stickers on their planners with their current National Curriculum, subdivided into thirds, for each subject. Thus for art one student had a level 3c. The student was asked what they needed to do: 'Get a 5b by next year' was the answer. 'How do you do that?', 'Work harder!'. This is not overly helpful as a target. Having a target is fine, if the pupil knows what to do to reach it.

As another example, consider a literal target, as in darts. I am useless at darts. When playing I was told 'Aim for the treble 20'. This is a real target, on a real board. Yet I have no idea how to do this. For me a more realistic target would be 'Try to hit the dartboard!'. What I need is a target involving how to hold the dart, how to throw it and what aiming it involves.

For the art student above this is the equivalent of being told to aim for the treble 20, when they need more specific help. Target setting needs to involve feedback, not be so general or vague as to be at worst pointless, and at best not helpful..

A criterion should be isolatable as much as possible

The idea here is that an item of assessment potential should be as uniquely definable as possible. Ideally this means that components of the whole can be deconstructed and determined individually. This takes us back to the issues of process and product. Sometimes the process is made visible, as when art students keep preliminary work and sketchbooks which show stages as to how the final product has been reached. Sometimes the process is all but invisible, for example when a poem is written in a flash of inspiration. Or take the case of a student composing a song. Here we would want to isolate assessment of the song's performance from the process of composing it, and not confuse or conflate the two.

Just because something is easy to assess does not mean it is worth assessing

There are things in artform-specific learning which are fairly straightforward to assess. Often these involve skills, paintbrush holding, mark-making, musical instrument technique, dance steps, dramatic gesture and so on. Assessing these is fine, if that is the *intention*, but the danger is to assume that assessing these gives an impression of the whole. In the example given, do we assume that brush-holding gives a view of the artistic merit of the picture as a whole? In the specific case of musical instrument technique, for example:

As I leave a concert, I have a clear notion of the quality of the performance which I have just heard. If someone asks me to justify my view, I may start to talk about rhythmic drive, or interpretation, or sense of ensemble, for instance. But I move from the whole performance to its components. I do not move from the components to the whole. In particular, I do not think: the notes were right, the rhythm was right, the phrasing was coherent, and so on – therefore I must have enjoyed this performance. And I certainly do not think something such as SKILLS + INTERPRETATION = PERFORMANCE

(Mills 2005: 176)

Even if there are things which are easily assessable in the classroom, does not mean they should be the only things which are assessed, which links to …

Just because something is hard to assess does not mean it should be ignored

Just as some things are easy to assess, some things are quite hard to assess. For instance, one of the key things that we will be looking for in student work in the arts is likely to be quality.

Reflective task

Try to write an assessment criterion that involves *quality* in any aspect of your teaching and learning.

Quality is notoriously hard to define, and concomitantly difficult to write assessment criteria for. As Pirsig observed:

Quality – you know what it is, yet you don't know what it is. But that's self-contradictory. But some things are better than others, that is, they have more quality. But when you try to say what the quality is, apart from the things that have it, it all goes poof! There's nothing to talk about. But if you can't say what Quality is, how do you know what it is, or how do you know that it even exists? If no one knows what it is, then for all practical purposes it doesn't exist at all. But for all practical purposes it really does exist. What else are the grades based on?

(Pirsig 1974: 178)

This is often the heart of the matter for assessment in the arts. Is this a worthwhile piece of artistic endeavour, a good picture/3D/sculpture/ composition/song/piece of theatre/ installation/video, or whatever? If so, should this not be represented in the assessment schedule? There are a number of ways this can be done, in cross-curricular teaching and learning work there may be more than one teacher involved, and so variations on Teresa Amabile's *consensual assessment technique* (Amabile 1996), can be employed. Recognising that finding assessment criteria for creativity is problematic, Amabile suggested instead using 'clearly subjective criteria' (1996: 34). What she proposes instead is to use a number of 'appropriate observers':

A product or response is creative to the extent that appropriate observers independently agree it is creative. Appropriate observers are those familiar with the domain in which the product was created or the response articulated. Thus, creativity can be regarded as the quality of products or responses judged to be creative by appropriate observers, and it can also be regarded as the process by which something so judged is produced.

(Amabile 1996: 33)

This enables the artform specific and general creative components of art-related work to be assessed for their quality in ways which do not simply become a single person's impression mark. Assessing quality in the arts is difficult, but if that is what is being aimed at, then it will be worth trying to tackle. Sometimes this can only be revealed in discussion with the students concerned. In the fascinatingly entitled '(In defence of) whippet-fancying and other vices: Re-evaluating assessment in art and design', Richard Hickman argues that:

If criteria are considered to be necessary ... the community decides on criteria for assessment, but we need to determine the size of the community; I would advocate that the learner's own criteria be used, which means that the community is a minimum of two people

(Hickman 2007: 84)

The implications of this are that quality can be discussed with the student, and evaluations arise from this discussion, and that one of the arbiters of this might well be the student concerned. This can be important where different responses are presented. Should the same criteria be used for a song, a picture, a poem, a dance, a play and a chest of drawers?

We have looked at the role of assessment criteria in helping to think about quality. But having criteria alone is not sufficient, they need to be shared with the students. We have already cited the work of D. Royce Sadler, one of the early writers on formative assessment, in Chapter 2, and it is worth restating in part here:

The indispensable conditions for improvement are that the student comes to hold a concept of quality roughly similar to that held by the teacher

(Sadler 1989: 121)

This means not only do the teachers need to establish a view as to what quality involves, but they also need to help the learners to understand this too. This can be a challenge, but if students do not know 'what a good one looks like', then potentially they will have trouble producing one!

Using assessment appropriately

What has come to be known as 'the standards agenda' has dominated thinking in educational circles over recent years, in the form of the National Curriculum and its associated testing and levelling regime, and Ofsted inspection for compliance. This has had a strong pull on assessment strategies, and it is only more recently that the much weaker push of formative assessment, AfL, has begun to make inroads into this. Faced with competing assessment pressures, we have seen how school assessment managers, often with a background in maths and the sciences, subjects which traditionally have had a closer alliance to summative assessment, have put pressure on the arts to adopt their methodologies, as Figure 6.4 shows.

The pressure shown in Figure 6.4 has put arts teachers under pressure, as one commented, 'When our school assessment co-ordinator asks to see my records, how am I going to be able to compete with the Maths and Science departments?' (Fautley 2004: 213). Arts teachers should not feel the need to compete, and these pressures need to be resisted. The weak push of formative assessment needs to take its place as *the* form of assessment which can make a difference to student learning, not only in the arts, but across the curriculum.

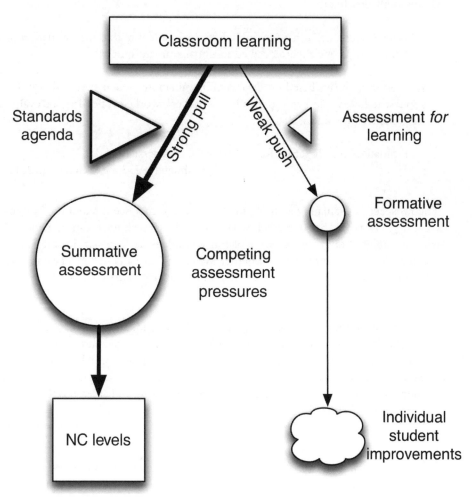

Figure 6.4 The pull and push of assessment (source: Fautley *et al.* 2008: 94).

From assessment to evaluation

We have considered so far the role of assessment. In the overarching book accompanying this, the role of evaluation is considered in some detail. The role of programme evaluation is seen as being very important, indeed, it is observed that 'the "educational project" of cross-curricular teaching and learning is in desperate need of educational evaluation' (Savage 2011: 156). Away from the United Kingdom, the terms assessment and evaluation go hand-in-hand, indeed, the United Kingdom is viewed with some concern by the Americans, for example, as programme (program) evaluation is not a normal part of teacher's work. A number of the examples of cross-curricular teaching and learning we have been discussing in this book, and in the accompanying books in this series, will be considered by many teachers to be novel, unusual or to require a different mode of delivery and experience. This means that where such programmes are run, teachers will want to undertake some form of evaluation. As the accompanying book notes, going on to cite Saville Kushner,

> in terms of outcomes, there is unlikely to be one 'truth' that the evaluation process will uncover. As one experienced educational evaluator put it:

> Evaluation is always based on data. Avoid evaluations which start with a judgement about whether a project was good or bad, whether it worked or not. In good evaluations, judgements grow out of that data.

> … Evaluation usually settles for something that is persuasive.
>
> (Kushner 1992: 3, cited in Savage 2011: 156)

The prospect of evaluating a cross-curricular course may seem daunting, but you will want to know what has succeeded, what can be developed, what can be reworked and what you might not do again. Some of this work does need to start in assessment. For example, you may want to know whether the pupils have attained in a fashion that is at least similar to what they might have done had the cross-curricular learning not taken place. Here are one teacher's comments on this:

> In terms of content knowledge, we baseline all our students when they come in. They have the test when they go out, a traditional test if you like, and I can see that their content knowledge is at least as good, if not better than it would have been normally. So I can be quite clear with my head of department, that actually all of the content they would normally get in Year 7, they are still getting and at least to the same level, if not to a higher level.
>
> (Fautley *et al.* 2008: 81)

This was useful in that the baseline assessment and then the end of unit test were used by this teacher to show his science colleagues that the cross-curricular work had not diluted science learning at all; indeed, as he notes, in this case he felt it was strengthened.

The key questions for cross-curricular programme evaluation are asked in the overarching book, and they are worth reiterating here:

1. Was this the appropriate time for a piece of curriculum development for me (as a teacher), for my pupils, my department, my school? How can I be sure?
2. What are the consequences of the changes I have made, on myself, my pupils and my colleagues?
3. How do the changes that I have advocated relate to other changes that we are being asked to make?
4. Where do the values come from that underpin this piece of curriculum development? Are they from my experiences or beliefs, or are they from somewhere else?
5. Who have been the winners and losers in this piece of curriculum development?
6. Has the teaching and learning been connected in this cross-curricular piece of curriculum development? How do you know?
7. How would you describe your teaching approach in this project? Has it been authoritarian or democratic, formal or informal? What aspects of my pedagogy have changed or developed from my traditional, subject-based pedagogy?
8. How have the pupils learnt in this project? In what ways have they learnt differently that they might have done in a more traditional approach to the same topic? What have you learnt by the whole experience?
9. Were my original aims, objectives and activities for the cross-curricular project appropriate? How did they change and develop over the duration of the project?
10. Whose knowledge really counts within a project like this? How did the knowledge base of my own subject specialism relate to other subjects that I was seeking to infuse within my teaching?
11. If this was a project that you did on your own, would it have worked better as a piece of collaborative curriculum development? If it was collaborative in its structure, can you conceive of it working more effectively as an independent activity? How could the collaborative dimensions of the project be translated into an individual teachers' pedagogical approach?

(Savage 2011: 164)

As is noted, not all of these questions will be appropriate for all projects, but they are worth considering nonetheless.

Evaluation of cross-curricular projects can also be undertaken using the seven-staged process of disciplined innovation proposed by the QCDA:

What are you trying to achieve?
1. Identify your priorities;
2. Record your starting point;
3. Set clear goals.

How will you organise learning?
    4. Design and implement.

How will you know when you are achieving your aims?
    5. Review progress;
    6. Evaluate and record the impact;
    7. Maintain, change or move on.

(QCDA 2009: 13–14)

However you and any colleagues involved in cross-curricular teaching and learning do it, programme evaluation will be a key feature of ongoing work in this area.

Storing and retrieving assessment data

> ### Reflective task
>
> How do you keep records at present?
>
> How much assessment data do your classes generate?
>
> How often do you enter assessment data?
>
> How often do you retrieve assessment data?.

There is little point in having assessment data of any sort, unless it makes sense and can be retrieved easily. Formative assessment, especially in the form of feedback, is particularly challenging to capture, but some teachers have managed this by getting pupils to make notes on conversations. These can then be written up, and entered onto appropriately designed documents often housed on the school's intranet, of which more later.

But formative assessment feedback and conversations are not the whole story. The work that the students do is also assessment data, in other words the plays, songs, pictures, sculptures, videos and so on. Storing these is clearly more problematic in some formats than others. How should a 3D sculpture be stored? In its original format, or as digital image on a computer? The same goes for a play. A play does not exist like a picture does, it is a performance event which happens in and over time. It can be recorded onto video: how is this stored, and how accessed? A short classroom play could last, say, for five minutes, over the course of a year many hours of video will be built up.

Classroom story

One drama teacher reckoned that all his annual holidays (without sleeping) could be spent watching the videos his students had made during the course of a year!

Is this reasonable?
How could it be managed?
Who watches it?
When?

There are clear issues for this amount of assessment data, and so it will be summarised levels, grades, and comments where storage of assessment data finds its most ready utility. But we need to distinguish again between formative and summative data. One music teacher makes audio recordings of students' work in progress performances every lesson, and then uses these as the starter activity for the next lesson. This is formative assessment data, and also acts as an aide memoire for the students. The many hours of audio that results need to be stored though, and again a problem can arise.

Practical task

Who has access to your assessment data?

What access to other teachers' assessment do you have?

Next time you access assessment data of any sort, think about where it is stored, and why you are accessing it. What will you do with it?.

Summative assessment is of a different order, as it is of a summary nature, and could just be a level or a grade. However, it is useful to remember that the summary grade is often a code for something, so a mark recorded as 'level 4' is shorthand for all of the level descriptor statements that accompanies it. Storing summative assessment data of this sort is considerably more straightforward than the audio, video and visual examples we have discussed above, and a pencil and a mark-book will often suffice!

However, the use of ICT for assessment data storage is becoming increasingly common in schools, and many schools run some form of data management system that relies on the regular entry of summative assessment data from teaching staff. This can seem like an imposition, but it is also worthwhile investigating the storage potential of the school's intranet. In the examples we have given, audio, video and visual data can be stored in digital form, and be instantly accessible. Digital file management systems often allow data to be 'tagged', and student names can be readily attached to files. This is particularly helpful in the case of the next area we shall consider, that of assessment in groups, and of group-work.

Assessment of groups and group-work

In Chapter 3 we investigated groups, and of social learning. In terms of assessment, groupwork can bring a problem, which is characterised by the question:

- Do I give everyone in the group the same mark?

Clearly this is a summative assessment question. Let us rephrase it in terms of formative assessment.

- Do I give everyone in the group the same feedback?

This seems more clear-cut. Individuated, personalised feedback is much more likely to be given when the teacher works with each group.

> ### Practical task
>
> Next time you and the students are undertaking groupwork try to listen to what you are saying! Are you giving generic feedback to the group, or are you targeting comments at individuals, or are you doing both?

There is not usually too much of an issue with giving personalised feedback, but it becomes a problem when a summative grade is given. Teachers have addressed this in a range of ways, including the use of self- and peer assessment when working in groups. We know that students require practice in peer-assessment techniques (Sebba 2006), but that when these are used well they can be very powerful. Some of the Assessing Pupils' Progress (APP) (National Strategies APP website n.d.) materials suggest concentrating on a few students for assessment purposes, in order to make the task manageable. This might be something that can be tried in cross-curricular teaching and learning programmes. We also need to return to the question asked in Figure 6.2 above, namely for whom is the assessment being undertaken? Boud's notion of double duty comes into play here too. Is the assessment trying to serve too many client groups? If it is fit for purpose for the students, is that good enough? If its only purpose is to generate levels for systemic purposes do the students need to be told? These situations need careful handling. What is important is that the assessment tail does not wag the cross-curricular teaching and learning dog!

Conclusion

Assessment and evaluation can be difficult and contentious areas of educational provision. In cross-curricular teaching and learning these problems are compounded by the fragmentary nature of National Curriculum assessment, the lack of clear guidelines on what is acceptable practice in terms of frequency of assessment, and a lack of clarity over what the purposes of some assessment data collection regimes are. Teachers involved in cross-curricular teaching and learning will need to find solutions which fit the wants and needs of their own particular circumstances, but always bearing in mind that one of the important aims of any assessment practice must be to help the students to improve their own learning.

Summary

This chapter has considered many of the issues associated with assessment in the arts. We have thought about differences between formative, summative and the formative use of summative data in assessment. We have considered what it means to write assessment criteria, and how these can be linked to learning outcomes in some cases. The problems associated with making assessment manageable have been introduced, and we have addressed ways in which this might be managed.

Meeting the Standards

This chapter will help you meet the following Q standards for ITT:
Q1, Q10, Q11, Q12, Q26a,b, Q27, Q28

Professional Standards for Teachers

This chapter will help you meet the following core standards:
C1, C10, C11, C12, C14,C26, C31, C32, C33, C34, C36

7

Looking forwards

Key objectives

By the end of this chapter, you will have:

- Reviewed the key themes of the book and applied them to your continuing professional development.

- Explored a metaphor for cross-curricular curriculum development which could underpin a new approach to cross-curricular teaching and learning in the arts.

- Identified aspects of your teaching pedagogy that will remain relevant and empowering in future educational scenarios.

Introduction

We are advocates for the arts in education. Everything we have said and written throughout this book is based on the premise that the arts are a vital part of every child's education. Nothing we have said should be seen or read to undermine this simple premise. Our discussions here have focused on how the arts can be linked together in imaginative ways, allowing common ideas, working processes and pedagogies to come together and learn from each other. Drawing on ideas developed within the companion title for this series of books (Savage 2011), Chapter 1 introduced the following definition for cross-curricular teaching and learning:

> A cross-curricular approach to teaching is characterised by sensitivity towards, and a synthesis of, knowledge, skills and understandings from various subject areas. These inform an enriched pedagogy that promotes an approach to learning which embraces and explores this wider sensitivity through various methods.

This definition is made up of two sets of three words: sensitivity, synthesis and subject; enrich, embrace and explore. There are some within the world of arts education who do not like the word 'subject'. Robinson, for example, considers the notion of the 'subject' to be a stifling concept, limiting creativity and acting as a barrier to innovation:

> We need to eliminate the existing hierarchy of subjects. Elevating some disciplines over others only reinforces outmoded assumptions of industrialism and offends the principle of diversity. The arts, sciences, humanities, physical education, languages and maths all have equal and central contributions to make to a student's education. … The idea of separate subjects that have nothing in common offends the principle of dynamism. School systems should base their curriculum not on the idea of separate subjects, but on the much more fertile idea of disciplines … which makes possible a fluid and dynamic curriculum that is interdisciplinary.
>
> (Robinson 2009)

Our argument throughout the book has been that school subjects should not be seen as separate from each other – conceptually, epistemologically or pedagogically. The physical differences between subjects within the secondary school (i.e. the organisation of spaces, classrooms, specialist teaching spaces etc.) may well enforce a significant degree of separation on how subjects relate to each other in the typical secondary school. But, although restructuring the curriculum along the lines of separate 'disciplines' may well be one way forward, it is a long way from where the majority of schools are at today. As we saw in Chapter 4, interdisciplinary is a term that has a special meaning for those working within the arts. It captures something of our ways of working as artists, musicians, dancers or actors and allows for natural links to be built between other areas of the curriculum, such as English. 'Cross-curricular', as a term, is one step removed from our work in that sense. But our arts subjects are part of the curriculum framework that we are dealing with today and seem likely to be with us for some time to come (although their exact shape or form may well change dramatically in the future). For this reason, our definition for cross-curricular teaching and learning talks about the importance of developing a sensitivity in our dealings with individual subject areas. In other words, making sure that we respect the subject cultures that underpin them, ensuring that they are handled with care. We know that for most teachers in the secondary school their sense of identity is inextricably linked to their subject and this cannot easily be untangled. There is also much of value in the historical approaches to how subjects have been taught within our schools that we would not want to lose. But a cross-curricular approach to teaching and learning in the arts implies that there has to be a synthesis of new ideas and approaches drawn from across the arts subjects. But it is more than this. As we have discussed throughout the book, the approaches to teaching and learning in the arts can extend beyond the arts and inform and develop other parts of the curriculum too. And, of course, the same is true in reverse. We have much to learn from the pedagogy and practices of science, the humanities, mathematics and all other curriculum areas. Hence our definitions of three 'E' words: embrace, explore and enrich. These characterise what we believe to be a positive approach to cross-curricular teaching and learning within and beyond the arts. One can take these words at face value: embrace other subjects, explore them and enrich your own teaching through them. Or one can treat them metaphorically and develop a whole new set of approaches for cross-curricular engagement. Either way, this is a positive approach that is located primarily within an individual teacher's pedagogy. This point is vital. Unlike many other materials and guidance on this issue, our book has not suggested that a cross-curricular approach to teaching and learning in the arts needs to solely depend on collaborations between teachers. We locate this approach at the level of the individual teacher, their way of thinking about their subject and the resultant pedagogy that they choose to develop. Collaborations may result and when they do, will be so much stronger for this original emphasis. Our final case study below will give one example of how a collaboration of this type was developed out of one teacher's innovative pedagogy. But this is not where true cross-curricular approaches to teaching and learning begin.

This chapter will not be able to predict, with any certainty, what the future of arts education holds within the United Kingdom. Future-gazing is notoriously difficult. But this chapter will consider a range of principles and practices for cross-curricular teaching and learning in the arts that will, we believe, ensure that this approach remains not just politically pertinent, but also becomes part of a coherent, educationally-justifiable, model of teaching and learning that has its roots in authentic artistic practices.

Practical task

Spend a few minutes flicking back through this book and any notes that you made in response to previous reflective or practical tasks. Can you identify or summarise the key ideas that have struck you through your reading to this point? Has your view on what constitutes a 'cross-curricular' approach to teaching and learning in the arts changed at all? Is there any evidence, however tentative, of a change in your own subject pedagogy as a result of engaging with the ideas in this book?

New approaches to cross-curricularity in the arts

Case studies have been an integral element within this book. Sharing stories about teaching and learning is an important process of teacher development. It is something that we all find valuable on those rare moments when we get time away from our classes to talk with other teachers. We can all think of interesting people from whom we have learnt in the past. Perhaps you know someone who always seems to have found an interesting website or teaching resource that they are using. As teachers we should value these relationships. Without them teaching becomes a very isolated activity. In our experience, this can lead to you becoming demoralised and ineffective as a teacher.

So for these reasons, we have tried throughout this book to provide a range of stories about curriculum projects and initiatives drawn from the work of a range of teachers. As we have stressed, these stories are included to demonstrate key points that we want to make. The majority of them, e.g. *Dunwich Revisited* (Chapter 4) and *Reflecting Others* (Chapter 5), have focused on the cross-curricular pedagogy of an individual teacher. These case studies are not there to be copied as approaches for cross-curricular teaching and learning in the arts. You will need to use the principles of this book, alongside other materials, to help develop your own pedagogy and practice within the local context of your school including, most importantly, the needs of the students that you teach.

This chapter will proceed with one final case study that is relevant to our overall theme of looking forward. It comes from a different type of school to the rest of our case studies. Egerton High School is a school for students with emotional and behavioural difficulties located in Trafford, a metropolitan borough in south-east Manchester. Each student at the school has been excluded from mainstream schooling in the borough. Class sizes are smaller than the average high school, and the opportunities for working creatively across the curriculum can be managed more easily. This story, featuring the work of the Head of Expressive Arts, describes how students were introduced to a new concept and technology (DubDubDub) that allowed them to manipulate the visual and audio elements of the Internet for a live performance.

CASE STUDY – The DubDubDub project

Audio exists on the Internet for a variety of reasons and serves a number of functions. It may arise incidentally by way of an embellishment to a corporate website or it may have a specific function such as a radio station. Sounds of the natural environment exist on the Internet and it is certainly easier to discover the sounds of a tropical rain forest on the Internet than organising the recording of these on location! There is a vast array of other sounds attached to web pages, many of which can be triggered through the control of a mouse. This interaction with a website can become part of the audio mix, e.g. the controlled output through clicking and triggering sounds with a mouse can feature alongside various embedded sounds that exist within the webpage.

The aim of DubDubDub was to develop an intuitive performance instrument for pupils that would facilitate the control of live Internet audio and visual materials. The prototype instrument, developed by a digital animator, was produced using Macromedia Flash. It allowed for Internet pages, along with embedded sounds, to be assigned to keys on the computer keyboard. As Figure 7.1 shows, each page could be opened or closed by pressing the appropriate key.

Pupils at Egerton High School tried out the initial DubDubDub interface. During this trial they commented that they had no problems using a standard Internet browser to open several web pages at a time on their desktop or keep them tabbed on the task bar. But this method highlighted some problems. Although it was easy to navigate the open web pages, using DubDubDub it was not always easy to find out which page was playing each audio element. In this method, there were just too many mouse clicks getting in the way of creating mixes and performing with Internet audio. Pupils also expressed their desire to display the video elements they found on certain pages. This initial interface did not allow them the opportunity to do this.

Figure 7.1 The initial DubDubDub interface.

During subsequent searches of the Internet for new browsers, a web browser was discovered that allowed for the tiling of pages within one page. The Avant Browser, (www.avantbrowser.com) was free to download and proved to be fast, stable, customisable and easy-to-use. Its use removed the need for the creation of a specific piece of DubDubDub software. Figure 7.2 shows four web pages open in one Avant Browser page. Please notice that the open pages are different searches from the Google Video site.

A very useful performance application of the Avant Browser facilitated the collection and storage of sets of favourite pages, enabling the user to return to them quickly in a live performance setting. The browser also facilitated the mixing of sounds as each 'tile' of a web page has controls for volume and looping its sonic content.

A second piece of software was combined with the Avant Browser for the DubDubDub project. Google Video (www.video.google.co.uk) is a dedicated video search engine that is content safe to use with pupils.

Figure 7.3 shows an open Google video on one Internet page. It is important to note the controls at the bottom of the page. These include a pause/play button, a time line cursor to locate or repeat sounds and a volume control slider. By

Figure 7.2 The Avant Browser.

Figure 7.3 The Google Video main page.

downloading the Google Video Player rather than just playing back videos within the Google video homepage, pupils were able to use these controls to facilitate a greater degree of versatility in terms of managing audio (as well as providing an enhanced quality of video playback). Figure 7.4 shows six videos open at once

Figure 7.4 Multiple Google Videos in the Avant Browser.

within the Avant Browser, each with controls accessible and a thumbnail of the selected video playing.

The combination of Google Video within the Avant Browser effectively provided pupils with a sound and vision mixing environment. The sonic environment of the Internet or specifically, in this case, the sounds attached to videos uploaded to Google Video, were manipulated and controlled by the DubDubDub player which is, itself, a conflation of existing technologies. The visual elements were controlled by simply maximising or minimising the various windows within the Avant Browser.

At this stage, the DubDubDub player was a facility consisting of a conflation of web technologies and a taught sensibility, a real time interactive tool and concept. Pupils needed a context to practice their new skills within. This led to a collaboration with a local university, Manchester Metropolitan University, and a performance within one of their faculty buildings.

Prior to the first performance with DubDubDub, a number of extended teaching sessions were held at Egerton High School. During these sessions, school pupils worked with a number of students from a local university who were undertaking a course of initial teacher education. These students formed a string quartet and worked with the school pupils to develop their skills with the DubDubDub player. During these sessions, the MCs (masters of ceremonies) and DJs (disc jockeys) shared their enthusiasm for music, demonstrated their skills and discussed ideas for the performance with the university students. There were many interesting conversations between the pupils and the students during these sessions

For the performance, the DubDubDub player was combined with a string quartet (formed by PGCE students from the university) and some MCs and DJs from Egerton High School. The first DubDubDub performance was given at a conference held within the university (Figure 7.5).

The performance moved through three sections. In the first section the string quartet played the opening section of Pachelbel's *Canon*. During the second stage of the performance, this was deconstructed as students moved away from their string instruments, one at a time, to add sounds and music using the DubDubDub interface on four Internet-enabled laptop computers. The resulting mix of sounds from the Internet formed the middle section of the performance. One student searched for Google Videos of violinists performing the same opening piece and this provided a simple conceptual link to the first section of the performance. Images from the browsers were displayed on a screen next to the performers. The final movement of the performance involved the MCs and DJs from Egerton High School. They introduced and blended in some contemporary grime beats using an MP3 player, a CD deck and a cross-fade mixer. Quite naturally they started spitting lyrics over the resulting sounds. Through these lyrics they introduced themselves, who they were reppin (representing) and established their style. Much of this was freestyling (a kind of vocal improvisation) combined with the inclusion of existing bars (sections of lyrics) that they had written to suit the occasion. During this final stage of the performance the string quartet/DubDubDub

Figure 7.5 The DubDubDub performance.

players gradually moved back to their string instruments from the laptops and improvised with the MCs and DJs. At the end of the performance all performers were contributing to the piece. The string players were improvising with the MCs and DJs and used the wider sonics and harmonics of their instruments to compliment the grime beats by emulating scratch sounds, sub-bass riffs, bass drum grooves and claps. The original baroque piece had been transformed through a DubDubDub-inspired breakdown into a unique presentation of improvised music and artistic expression.

A more detailed account of the DubDubDub project can be read in Savage and Butcher (2007).

The story of DubDubDub has many lessons for future approaches to cross-curricular teaching and learning in the arts.

1. Artistic processes can empower cross-curricular practices

At a fundamental level, all arts subjects are concerned with artistic processes and products. One of the key successes of the DubDubDub project was to allow students (from the university and the school) to engage with musical and artistic processes through a range of resources (their traditional instruments and modern technologies). There were a number of different combinations here. First, students from two very different academic institutions found a common artistic cause to unite within. Second, classical music met with contemporary dance music. Third, modern day technologies merged with classical instruments. Finally, the artistic process combined with the artistic product. The artistic process unfolded in the eyes and ears of the audience, in real time; the artistic process itself being facilitated by the combined improvisational approaches adopted by all involved.

These combinations translate, metaphorically and beautifully, to the arguments presented within this book. Curriculum subjects, like the groups of students involved in the DubDubDub project, are, by nature and experience, very different. They have different priorities and concerns; they look, and speak, very differently. Their styles of teaching and learning are equally varied and distinctive. These become embodied in the pedagogies of different teachers; some have a more traditional approach, others are more contemporary in their practice. As with the technologies in the DubDubDub project, the tools we use in our teaching vary considerably. Some teachers are more familiar, and skilful, with what might be called 'classical' tools; others respond better and are more at ease with the blend of newer technologies that the digital era has made available. Ultimately, the processes of teaching and learning that fill our classrooms are related to the 'products' of learning. Defining what the 'product' of an education experience ought to be is difficult. But the artistic processes at play here can help make the process of teaching and learning in the arts more transparent. Taking time to savour and enjoy them is a key lesson the arts can give to the wider curriculum subjects.

2. Enhancing the subject: one plus one equals three (or more)

All artists know that one plus one equals more than two! When two objects are bought together into the same frame, the resulting impact on the artist and viewer is significantly more that either of the two objects considered independently. A relationship is established between the objects that extends each further than it could have gone on its own. Although music was the main focus of the DubDubDub performance, having a screen that presented the decisions about which websites the DubDubDub players decided to visit created some transparency for the audience and demystified the sources of sounds. In Buxton's terms (Buxton 2005: 5) it provided the audience with a visible side to musical cause and effect. Through discussion after the performance, it was apparent that it enriched the audience's appreciation of the skills and control of the sounds that the players were manipulating. This is equivalent to watching a string player's physical manipulation of their instrument. Using the DubDubDub player is, by nature, an audio and visual experience. It allows the user to cut up culture, rearrange and subvert images, video and sounds live from the Internet to create new and unique audio or visual 'instances'. Whether the user is dealing with sonic or visual elements, or both, the DubDubDub player facilitated artistic expression through the sonic and visual environment of the Internet, honing an appreciation of the role of chance in the artistic endeavour.

One of the potential benefits of cross-curricular teaching and learning may be that the potential of the combined subjects is greater than that of any of the individual parts. Whilst this statement needs further research, the lessons from DubDubDub and other artistic collaborations like it are that combining art forms results in a greater sense of clarity and distinctiveness in terms of the chosen artistic processes that are undertaken. But beyond that, the combinations allow for a playfulness around the edges of the subjects that can bring in much more of value for teaching and learning processes then those achieved by an insular, subject-orientated approach.

3. Engagement, inclusion and immediacy

As a concept, DubDubDub demonstrates that cross-curricular approaches work in terms of increasing pupil engagement and inclusion in the arts. One of the most attractive aspects of the project for us was the quality of interactions between pupils at the school and the university students. These even included the occasion impromptu violin lessons for the pupils! Within the context of this school, this type of openness, communication and exchange was quite remarkable and took the teacher by surprise.

Again, these reflections help promote a positive approach to cross-curricular teaching and learning in the arts with certain distinctive features. First, the simplicity of the tools developed and used in the project allowed pupils immediate engagement. They allowed the pupils access to a range of artistic processes that captured their imaginations quickly. All pupils could get involved. Unlike a classical string instrument which is hard to play and takes years to master, these pupils could partake in the processes of artistic creation quickly. But much more importantly that this simple notion of engagement and immediacy, the combinations that we spoke about under Section 1, above, resulted in genuine, meaningful and authentic artistic collaborations between all participants, despite (or perhaps that is because of?) their very different backgrounds.

DubDubDub pays homage to many different forms of artistic expression. One of these was John Cage's *Roaratorio*. This work consists of a number of elements, including the reading of Cage's specially prepared text, Irish ballads, jigs and instrumental music played by groups of musicians, and recorded materials (in total over 2,293 sounds) which depict locations and noises that appear in *Finnegan's Wake* (a book of comic fiction written by James Joyce). These sounds include thunderclaps, thunder rumbles, earthquake sounds, laughing, crying, bells, clocks, chimes and much more besides. *Roaratorio*, constructed by Cage in 1979, was composed without the benefits of modern sampling techniques or, of course, the Internet! His statement that, 'I never imagine anything until I experience it' is hugely relevant in this context (Cage 2007). It is this sensibility to the spontaneous and immediate working with artistic materials that Cage demonstrated so effectively in his own work that became central to the DubDubDub performance. It was pleasing to note that this concept, complete with its technological, visual and musical dimensions, promoted the artistic appreciation of two very diverse groups of young people. Not only that, but it brought them together to share an artistic discourse which, we believe, it would have been hard to imagine through any other means.

By now, we hope, the point is obvious. As arts educators we have a responsibility to encourage this playful approach to cross-curricularity because it is an intrinsic part of what we do as artists. How do you sum up what you do as an artist? Here is our attempt: we put things together, craft and build, edit and experiment, take things and relocate them, find meaning in things (sometimes in the meaningless), touch, feel, explore and create; we cherish and embellish, recreate and enhance, express, regress and, on occasions, digress. But surely creativity is central to everything we do. Our approach to teaching, learning and curriculum development should be as rich as are our artistic endeavours in this respect. It is this thought that leads us on to the final part of our book.

Reflective task

Our analysis of DubDubDub has highlighted several key benefits of cross-curricular approaches to teaching and learning in the arts. Spend time reflecting on the following questions:

1. To what extent can key artistic processes drawn from other arts subjects help empower my own subject pedagogy?

2. How can the enriched cross-curricular pedagogy that we develop help extend our work further into other subjects within the curriculum?

3. Issues of engagement, inclusion and immediacy are important within all subjects. What specific aspects of my subject pedagogy could be enhanced by the development of cross-curricular links of the types illustrated by the DubDubDub case study?

A creative approach to curriculum development

As teachers, we need to rediscover the concept of curriculum development. For many teachers, the curriculum is developed elsewhere (i.e. the National Curriculum, or a GCSE specification, covers that element of their work). It is because of this viewpoint that we say it needs to be rediscovered. Curriculum development, in our view, is something that teachers do. Right at the beginning of Chapter 1, we explored this notion of the curriculum and what it means for the individual teacher. We reasserted Stenhouse's view, that there is 'no curriculum development without teacher development' (Stenhouse 1980: 85).

In the accompanying title to this book (Savage 2011), a number of different curriculum 'types' were explored. Taking a cue from Ross' use of the term 'Baroque' as a metaphor to describe a curriculum which contains 'clearly demarcated subjects, classified by both content knowledge and by the discourse forms appropriate and specific to each discipline' (Ross 2000: 3), a 'Renaissance' metaphor for the curriculum was developed. Renaissance scholars have identified two themes that are pertinent to the possible formation of a 'Renaissance' curriculum model (Cassirer 2000; Kristeller 1990). First, the theme of universal orderliness; second, the theme of universal interdependence. Universal orderliness was premised on the concept that every existing thing in the universe had its place in a divinely planned hierarchical order; universal interdependence held the belief that different segments of this great chain of universal orderliness reflected each other in particular ways in what were known as 'correspondences'. As an example, Renaissance thinkers viewed a human being as being a microcosm of the world as a whole. As the world was comprised for four elements (earth, water, air and fire), therefore the human body was composed of four 'humours' (sanguine, choleric, phlegmatic and melancholy). This had implications for medical science, philosophy and psychology within the period.

The existing curriculum models that permeate schools today could be conceived as presenting an orderly model of subjects, arranged in a hierarchical structure of sorts by perceived academic value (hence we have core or foundation subjects; optional or compulsory subjects at particular ages) akin to Ross' Baroque curriculum model (Ross 2000: 3). For each subject culture within this model, there will be categorisations or levels of knowledge, skills and understanding which are valued, perhaps some more highly than others. As we are only too aware, the arts subjects are often undervalued within schools when placed against other curriculum subjects in this model.

But within the cross-curricular Renaissance curriculum model, the notions of universal interdependence and correspondences become the metaphors for cross-curricularity and a different way of thinking about how subjects relate to each other. They facilitate exchanges or correspondences between subjects that relate to and enforce the natural orderliness found within the particular subject cultures. Whilst there will not be exact parallels (and this is where the metaphor begins to fall down), teachers' sensitivity to working across and between the subjects in this way begins to promote an orderliness in knowledge, thinking and understanding which may help stimulate students' cross-curricular learning and, perhaps, help them situate their learning within ways of thinking that are more closely related to their wider life experiences.

The idea of a 'Renaissance' model of cross-curricular development can be further enhanced when one investigates more closely the nature of the arts in the Renaissance period. For example, the music of the Renaissance period is characterised by polyphony, where composers wrote for many voices as if they were one. They did this by:

- Sharing common melodic materials between the voices.

- Allowing different voices to take the lead at different times.

- Ensuring that the voices were equally important and that one voice did not dominate the music at any given point.

- Handling dissonance (i.e. what could be perceived as 'clashes' in the sound of the music at a particular point) in a specific way, making sure that any of these tensions in the music were both prepared and resolved for the listener.

What would this metaphor of polyphony look like in our Renaissance model for cross-curricular curriculum development? It would allow the individual teacher to take key knowledge, skills and understanding, which are initiated and developed by individual subjects (the voices), and share these in a way that allows them to exist alongside each other with an equal sense of value. Within the context of their own teaching, it would allow a particular subject perspective to take the lead at a particular times, but always within a combined, overall sense of balance, purpose and direction that is in relationship to the whole. Perhaps a specific theme would be highlighted for a certain period and then developed by the various subject perspectives, each one presenting it with its own particular tone or resonance. It could handle potential clashes of knowledge or learning by carefully preparing learners for the potential dissonance, allowing them to enjoy the creative tension that the dissonance allows before resolving it for them in a sensitively managed and appropriate way.

Reflective task

Creative and metaphorical thinking of the type that underpins the cross-curricular renaissance curriculum model is a useful way of exploring new possibilities for the organisation of teaching and learning. But what about your role as a teacher in all of this? What are the metaphors that you could apply to your own work and the development of a cross-curricular pedagogy within it? As an example, the accompanying title to this book (Savage 2011) explores metaphors such as whether you may be a 'hedgehog or a fox' in your thinking, or whether your teaching is characterised by a 'centrifugal' or 'centripetal' approach.

Ultimately, a Renaissance curriculum is one of many potential metaphors that could encourage a sympathetic approach to cross-curricular teaching and learning in the arts. Perhaps you can think of your own? But it is time to turn our attention briefly to the second, key part of these concluding thoughts. What style of teaching would facilitate such a model?

What type of teacher do you want to be?

This book closes with a simple question. What type of teacher to do you want to be? Perhaps you are reading this book at the beginning of your teaching career. You have the opportunity to make choices about the type of teacher you want to be and start as you mean to go on. Or perhaps you have a number of years teaching under your belt already. You are comfortable, skilful and successful at what you do. Either way, we do not believe that this a time to be complacent. The next twenty years holds significant challenges for our work as teachers.

In our opinion, the concepts of individual subjects have a limited currency in education. In the short term, they will remain as an organising principle. But an analysis of recent changes in the curriculum show these being replaced by more generic curriculum themes and approaches on a regular basis already. Within these changes, subject knowledge still plays an important part and teachers are able to react and reorganise their approaches with minimal impact on their pedagogy and practice. But we do not think this will be the case for too much longer. More significant changes to curriculum design and implementation will emerge which stretch the traditional organising principles of subjects and subject cultures to breaking point. Subjects in the curriculum, at least in the way that we have them today, may cease to exist. Subject specialists will need to re-think the ways in which subject knowledge contributes to these new curriculum and pedagogical frameworks.

So, how are you going to respond to the challenges contained within this book and, more importantly, the changing landscape of education within our schools? Does cross-curricular teaching and learning in the arts have a future within your pedagogy and practice? Ultimately, you will have to decide. We will conclude this book with some things that we know to be true.

First, formal, top-down policy initiatives for greater degrees of cross-curricular activities within schools have failed. History has taught us that. If a meaningful, sustainable and systematic cross-curricular approach to teaching and learning is going to succeed, it needs to be reborn and resituated within the pedagogy of individual teachers.

Second, within the context of the majority of secondary schools, the notion of the subject specialist, and the accompanying subject cultures, are firmly established in curricular and assessment frameworks. There will need to be a major shift in pedagogical thinking and practice for this to change.

Third, timescales are always difficult to predict. It seems likely that a shift towards a meaningful reorganisation of the secondary school, perhaps along the lines envisaged by Ken Robinson (Robinson 2009), will only take place in the medium to long term. In the shorter term, individual teachers will need to make decisions about the organisation and delivery of a cross-curricular curriculum offering within their own teaching.

We are optimistic that teachers will rise to the challenge and, providing the key principles that we have explored together within this book are adhered to, the possibility for an authentic cross-curricular approach to teaching and learning in the arts emerging seems strong. One of the keys for our work over the next few years will be to find appropriate platforms for the sharing of successful approaches to cross-curricular teaching and learning. Alongside his remit that there is no curriculum development without teacher development, Lawrence Stenhouse had another famous aphorism, 'research is systematic enquiry *made public*' [emphasis added] (Stenhouse 1983: 11). Whilst our call is for individual teachers to take ownership of cross-curricular approaches to teaching and learning within their teaching, an important aspect of this will be how they formulate, share and discuss the stories of their emerging practices in this area. The activities of educational research may be appropriate for some. Commitments to advanced level postgraduate study will suit others. But all teachers need time and space to collaborate on developing their own cross-curricular, subject-based pedagogy before they can be expected to take part in meaningful cross-curricular collaborations with other colleagues.

Professional Standards for QTS

This chapter will help you meet the following Q standards: Q6, Q7a, Q8, Q10, Q11, Q14.

Professional Standards for Teachers

This chapter will help you meet the following core standards: C6, C7, C8, C15, C16, C30, C40, C41.

Links to other books in this series

We hope you have enjoyed reading this title. This book is one of a series of books published by Routledge investigating cross-curricular approaches to teaching and learning. The generic series title, *Cross-Curricular Teaching and Learning in the Secondary School*, written by Dr Jonathan Savage, takes an overall look at the issues of cross-curricular teaching and learning in the secondary school. The other titles take a detailed look at the possibilities of developing a cross-curricular approach within each of six different disciplinary areas. Each takes a predominantly practical approach to issues that have been raised here. As such, we urge you to explore these ideas further through these accompanying titles:

- *Cross-Curricular Teaching and Learning in the Secondary School ...English*
- *Cross-Curricular Teaching and Learning in the Secondary School ...Mathematics*
- *Cross-Curricular Teaching and Learning in the Secondary School ...Science*
- *Cross-Curricular Teaching and Learning in the Secondary School ... the Humanities*
- *Cross-Curricular Teaching and Learning in the Secondary School ...Modern Foreign Languages*
- *Cross-Curricular Teaching and Learning in the Secondary School ...ICT*

Bibliography

Abbs, P (1982) *English Within the Arts: A Radical Alternative for English and the Arts in the Curriculum*, London: Hodder & Stoughton.

—— (2003) *Against the Flow: Education, the Arts and Postmodern Culture*, London: RoutledgeFalmer.

Alexander, R. (2004) Still no pedagogy? Principle, pragmatism and compliance in primary education, *Cambridge Journal of Education*, 34(1): 7–33.

Alexander, R. J. (2008) *Essays on Pedagogy*, London: Routledge.

Amabile, T. (1996) *Creativity in Context*, Boulder, CO: Westview Press.

Apple (2009) online, available at: http://www.apple.com/iphone/appstore/ [accessed 20 March 2009].

Assessment Reform Group (2002) *Assessment for Learning: 10 Principles*, online, available at: www.assessment-reform-group.org/CIE3.pdf [accessed 18 July 2010].

Baldwin, P. and Fleming, K. (2003) *Teaching Literacy Through Drama: Creative Approaches*, London: RoutledgeFalmer.

Bandura, A. (1986) *Social Foundations of Thought and Action: A Social Cognitive Theory*, Englewood Cliffs, NJ: Prentice-Hall.

—— (1993) Perceived self-efficacy in cognitive development and functioning, *Educational Psychologist*, 28(2): 117–48.

Berger, J. (1972) *Ways of Seeing*, Harmondsworth: Penguin.

Bernstein, B. (1971) On the classification and framing of educational knowledge, in M. Young (ed.), *Knowledge and Control*, London: Collier-Macmillan, pp. 47–69.

—— (1999) Official knowledge and pedagogic identities, in F. Christie (ed.) *Pedagogy and the Shaping of Consciousness*, London: Cassell.

Bloom, B.S. (1956) *Taxonomy of Educational Objectives, Handbook I: The Cognitive Domain*, New York: David McKay Co Inc.

——, Krathwohl, D. and Masia, B. (1964) *Taxonomy of Educational Objectives: Book 2: Affective Domain*, New York: David McKay & Co.

Boden, M.A. (1990) *The Creative Mind: Myths and Mechanisms*, London: Weidenfeld and Nicolson.

Bolton, G.M. (1998) *Acting in Classroom Drama: A Critical Analysis*, Stoke-on-Trent: Trentham in association with the University of Central England.

Boud, D. (2000) Sustainable assessment: rethinking assessment for the learning society, *Studies in Continuing Education*, 22(2): 151–67.

Bowers, C. (1993). *Critical Essays on Education, Modernity, and the Recovery of the Ecological Imperative*, New York: Teachers' College Press.

Bresler, L. (1995) The subservient, co-equal, affective, and social integration styles and their implications for the arts, *Arts Education Policy Review*, 96(5): 31–7.

Bruner, J. (1966) *Toward a Theory of Instruction*, Cambridge, MA: Harvard University Press.

—— (1996) *The Culture of Education*, Cambridge, MA: Harvard University Press.

Buxton, B. (2005) *Causality and Striking the Right Note*, Proceedings of the 2005 International Conference on New Interfaces for Music Expression, Vancouver, BC, Canada.

Cage, J. (2007) Roaratorio: *An Irish Circus on Finnegan's Wake, For Voice, Tape and Irish Musicians*, online, available at: http://www.answers.com/topic/roaratorio-an-irish-circus-on-finnegan-s-wake-for-voice-tape-irish-musicians?cat=entertainment [accessed 4 July 2007].

Cain, T. (2004) Theory, technology and the music curriculum, *British Journal of Music Education*, 21(2): 215–21.

Cassirer, E. (2000) *The Individual and the Cosmos in Renaissance Philosophy*, New York: Dover Publications.

Chaiklin, S. (2003) The zone of proximal development in Vygotsky's analysis of learning and instruction, in A. Kozulin, B. Gindis, V.S. Ageyev and S.M. Miller (eds), *Vygotsky's Educational Theory in Cultural Context*, Cambridge: Cambridge University Press, pp. 39–64.

Claxton, G., Pollard, A. and Sutherland, R. (2003) Fishing in the fog: conceptualising learning at the confluence of cultures, in R. Sutherland, G. Claxton and A. Pollard (eds) *Learning and Teaching: Where World Views Meet*, London: Trentham Books.

Cohen, L., Manion, L. and Morrison, K. (2004) *A Guide to Teaching Practice*, fifth edition, London: RoutledgeFalmer.

Craft, A. (2003) The limits to creativity in education: dilemmas for the educator, *British Journal of Educational Studies*, 51(2): 113–27.

Daniels, H. (2004) Activity theory, discourse and Bernstein, *Educational Review*, 56(2): 121–32.

DfEE (1997) *Connecting the Learning Society*, London: DfEE.

DfES (2002) *Training Materials for the Foundation Subjects*, London: DfES.

—— (2006) *Secondary National Strategy: Foundation Subjects: KS3 Music Unit 1: Structuring Learning for Musical Understanding*, Norwich: DfES.

Dhomont, F. (2002). *My Cinema for the Ears*, (DVD) Bridge Records Inc.

Draper, P. (2008) Music two-point-zero: music, technology and digital independence, *Journal of Music, Technology and Education*, 1(2–3): 137–52.

Efland, A. (2002) *Art and Cognition: Integrating the Visual arts in the Curriculum*, New York: Teachers' College Press.

Eikenberry, K. (2009) *The Kevin Eikenberry Group*, online, available at: www.kevineikenberry.com [accessed 5 January 2010].

Eisner, E. (1985) *The Art of Educational Evaluation: A Personal View*, London/ New York: The Falmer Press.

—— (1987) Celebration of Thinking, *Educational Horizons*, 66(1): 1–4.

—— (2002) *The Arts and the Creation of Mind*, New Haven/London: Yale University Press.

Engeström, Y., Miettenen, R. and Punamaki, R.L. (eds) (1999) *Perspectives on Activity Theory*, Cambridge: Cambridge University Press.

Eraut, M. (2001) Non-formal learning, implicit learning and tacit knowledge in professional work, in F. Coffield (ed.) *The Necessity of Informal Learning*, Bristol: The Policy Press.

Facer, K. (2009) *Educational, Social and Technological Futures: A report from the Beyond Current Horizons Programme*, London: DCSF and Futurelab.

Fautley, M. (2004) Teacher intervention strategies in the composing processes of lower secondary school students, *International Journal of Music Education*, 22(3): 201–18.

—— (2007) Lost in translation: the changed language of assessment in music education, *NAME Journal*, Summer: 2–4.

—— (2010) *Assessment in Music Education*, Oxford: Oxford University Press.

—— and Savage, J. (2008) *Assessment for Learning and Teaching in Secondary Schools*, Exeter: Learning Matters.

——, Hatcher, R. and Millard, E. (in press) *Remaking the Curriculum: Re-engaging Young People in Secondary School*, Stoke on Trent: Trentham Books.

—— , Gee, M., Hatcher, R. and Millard, E. (2008) *The Creative Partnerships Curriculum Projects at Kingstone School Barnsley and Queensbridge School Birmingham*, Research Report, Birmingham: Birmingham City University, online, available at: www.creativitycultureeducation.org/data/files/kingstone-and-queensbridge-2008-100.pdf.

FMS (2010) *Wow, It's Music Next*, online available at: www.thefms.org [accessed 1 February 2010].

Fennell, M. and Jenkins, H. (2004) Low self-esteem, in J. Bennett-Levy, G. Butler, M. Fennell, A. Hackmann, M. Mueller and D. Westbrook (eds), *Oxford Guide to Behavioural Experiments in Cognitive Therapy*, new York: Oxford University Press.

Fitzsimmons, C. (2009) Government Outlines Digital Rights Agency Proposal, *The Guardian*, 13 March 2009, online, available at: www.guardian.co.uk/media/2009/mar/13/uk-government-outlines-digital-rights-agency [accessed 20 March 2009].

Foucault, M. (1979) *Discipline and Punish: The birth of the Prison*, New York: Vintage.

Frankel, J. (2010) *The iPad in Music Education: First Impressions*, online, available at: www.jamesfrankel.musiced.net/2010/01/30/the-ipad-in-music-education-first-impressions [accessed 1 February 2010].

Futurelab (2006) *Teachers' Learning with Digital Technologies: A Review of Research and Projects*, Bristol: Futurelab, online, available at: www.futurelab.org.uk/resources [accessed 20 October 2009].

Gadsden, V. (2008) The arts and education: knowledge generation, pedagogy, and the discourse of learning, *Review of Research in Education*, 32(1): 29–61.

Galison, P. (1997) *Image and Logic: The Material Culture of Micro-Physics*, Chicago: University of Chicago Press.

Gardner, H. (1998) Foreword: complementary perspectives on Reggio Emilia, in C. Edwards and L. Gandini (eds), *The Hundred Languages of Children: The Reggio Emilia Approach – Advanced Reflections*, Westport CT: Ablex Publishing Corporation.

—— (2006) *The Development and Education of the Mind: The Selected Works of Howard Gardner*, London: Routledge.

Gee, M. (in press) The contribution of drama, in M. Fautley, R. Hatcher and E. Millard (eds), *Remaking the Curriculum: Re-engaging Young People in Secondary School*, Stoke on Trent: Trentham Books.

Gilbert, C. and Teaching and Learning in 2020 Review Group (2006) *2020 Vision: Report of the Teaching and Learning in 2020 Review Group*, London: DfES.

Gillborn, D. (2000) Anti-racism: from policy to praxis, in B. Moon M. Ben-Peretz and S. Brown (eds), *Routledge International Companion to Education*, London: Routledge.

Glynn, S. and Takahashi, T. (1998) Learning from analogy-enhanced science texts, *Journal of Research in Science Teaching*, 35(10): 1129–49.

Goehr, L. (1992) *The Imaginary Museum of Musical Works*, Oxford: Clarendon Press.

Goodson, I.F. and Mangen, J.M. (1998) Subject cultures and the introduction of classroom computers', in I.F. Goodson (ed.) *Subject Knowledge: Readings for the Study of School Subjects*, London: Falmer Press.

Gorden, D. (1978) *Therapeutic Metaphors*, Cupertino, CA: Meta.

Graham, F. (2009) *Disability No Barrier to Gaming*, London: BBC, online, available at: http://news.bbc.co.uk/1/hi/technology/7935336.stm [accessed 20 March 2009].

Green, L. (2000) Music as media art, in J. Sefton-Green (ed.), *Evaluating Creativity*, London: RoutledgeFalmer.

Gruhn, W. and Rauscher, F. (2006) The neurobiology of music cognition and learning, in R. Colwell (ed.), *MENC Handbook of Musical Cognition and Development*, New York: Oxford University Press, pp. 40–71.

Hale, J. (2007) *A Guide to Curriculum Mapping: Planning, Implementing, and Sustaining the Process*, Thousand Oaks, CA: Corwin Press.

Hall, K. and Harding, A. (2002) Level descriptions and teacher assessment in England: towards a community of assessment practice, *Educational Research Review*, 44(1): 1–16.

Hargreaves, D.H. (1991) Coherence and manageability: reflections on the National Curriculum and cross-curricular provision, *Curriculum Journal*, 2(1): 33–41.

Harland, J., Lord, P., Stott, A., Kinder, K., Lamont, E. and Ashworth, M. (2005) *The Arts-Education Interface: A Mutual Learning Triangle?* Slough: NFER.

Harlen, W. (2005) Teachers' summative practices and assessment for learning: tensions and synergies, *Curriculum Journal*, 16(2): 207–23.

—— and James, M. (1997) Assessment and learning: differences and relationships between formative and summative assessments, *Assessment in Education*, 4(3): 365–79.

Heppell, S. (2010) *Playful Learning's the Answer. What is the question?* http://agent4change.net/index.php?option=com_content&view=article&id=492:playful-learnings-the-answer-whats-the-question&catid=98:innovation&Itemid=478 [accessed 6 January 2010].

Hickman, R. (2007) (In defence of) whippet-fancying and other vices: re-evaluating assessment in art and design, in T. Rayment (ed.), *The Problem of Assessment in Art and Design*, Bristol: Intellect Books.

Hoffman, R. (1983) Recent research on metaphor, *Semiotic Inquiry*, 3: 35–62.

Hughes, A. (2002) Reconceptualising the art curriculum, *Journal of Art and Design Education*, 17(1): 41–9.

Hymas, C. (1991) The great composers expelled from school, *The Sunday Times,* London.

James, M. (2006) Assessment, teaching and theories of learning, in J. Gardner (ed.), *Assessment and Learning,* London: Sage.

Jenkins, H., Purushotma, R., Clinton, K., Weigel, M. and Robison, A.J. (2007) *Confronting the Challenges of Participatory Culture: Media Education for the 21st Century*, an occasional paper on digital media and learning, Chicago, IL: The MacArthur Foundation, online, available at: http://digitallearning.macfound.org/atf/cf/%7B7E45C7E0-A3E0-4B89-AC9C-E807E1B0AE4E%7D/JENKINS_WHITE_PAPER.PDF.

Jephcote, M. and Davies, B. (2007) School subjects, subject communities and curriculum change: the social construction of economics in the school curriculum, *Cambridge Journal of Education*, 37(2): 207–27.

Jerram, L. (2009) *Play Me, I'm Yours*, online, available at: www.lukejerram.com/projects/play_me_im_yours [accessed 12 December 2009].

John, P. (2005) The sacred and the profane: subject sub-culture, pedagogical practice and teachers' perceptions of the classroom uses of ICT, *Educational Review*, 57(4): 469–88.

John-Steiner, V. (1997) *Notebooks of the Mind: Explorations of Thinking*, revised edition, New York: Oxford University Press.

Kalantzis, M. and Cope, B. (2008) *New Learning: Elements of a Science of Education*, Cambridge: Cambridge University Press.

Kelly, A.V. (2009) *The Curriculum: Theory and Practice*, sixth edition, London: Sage.

Kristeller, P.O. (1990) *Renaissance Thought and the Arts*, Princeton, NJ: Princeton University Press.

Kushner, S. (1992) *The Arts, Education and Evaluation: An Introductory Pack with Practical Exercises Section 1: Introduction*, Norwich: Centre for Applied Research in Education, University of East Anglia.

Kutnick, P., Blatchford, P. and Baines, E. (2005) Grouping of pupils in secondary school classrooms: possible links between pedagogy and learning, *Social Psychology of Education,* 8(4): 349–74.

Lakoff, G. and Johnson, M. (1981) *Metaphors We Live By*, Chicago: Chicago University Press.

Lave, J. and Wenger, E. (1991) *Situated Learning: Legitimate Peripheral Participation*, Cambridge: Cambridge University Press.

Lucas, B. and Claxton, G. (2010) *New Kinds of Smart - How the Science of Learning Intelligence is Changing Education*, Maidenhead: Open University Press.

Mansell, W., James, M. and Assessment Reform Group (2009) *Assessment in schools. Fit for purpose? A Commentary by the Teaching and Learning Research Programme*, London: Economic and Social Research Council, Teaching and Learning Research Programme.

Mansilla, V. and Gardner, H. (2009) Disciplining the mind, in M. Scherer (ed.), *Challenging the Whole Child: Reflections on Best Practices in Learning, Teaching, and Leadership*, Alexandria, VA: ASCD, pp. 97–107.

Marzano, R. and Kendall, J. (2007) *The New Taxonomy of Educational Objectives*, Thousand Oaks, CA: Corwin Press.

Maslow, A. (1954) *Motivation and Personality*, New York: Harper & Row.

Maur, K. (1999) *The Sound of Painting: Music in Modern Art*, London/New York: Prestel.

Mills, J. (1991) *Music in the Primary School*, Cambridge: Cambridge University Press.

—— (2005) *Music in the School*, Oxford: Oxford University Press.

MoE website (n.d.) *What is moe?* online, available at: www.mantleoftheexpert.com/about-moe/introduction/what-is-moe [accessed March 2010].

Moon, B. (1995) The National Curriculum: origins, context and implementation, in B. Moon and A. Shelton Mayes (eds), *Teaching and Learning in the Secondary School*, London: Routledge, pp. 245–60.

—— and Murphy, P. (1999) Perspectives on the Context of Curriculum, in B. Moon and P. Murphy (eds), *Curriculum in Context*, London: Paul Chapman.

Morrison, R. (1991) A generation drummed out, *The Times*, London.

NACCCE (1999) *All Our Futures: Creativity, Culture and Education* Sudbury: DfEE.

NASAGA (2009) *Creating Metaphors and Analogies to Use in Training and Other Learning Events*, online, available at: www.laurelandassociates.com/pdfs/creating_metaphors.pdf [accessed 15 December 2009].

National Strategies (2006) *Introducing Tasks to Groups*, online, available at: http://nationalstrategies. standards.dcsf.gov.uk/node/84689 [accessed March 2010].

National Strategies APP Website (n.d.), *Assessing Pupils' Progress*, online, available at: http://nationalstrategies.standards.dcsf.gov.uk/search/primary/results/nav:80988 [accessed March 2010].

NCC (1989) *Circular No. 6*, York: NCC.

Ofsted (2009a) *Drawing Together: Art, Craft and Design in Schools 2005-8*, London: Ofsted.

—— (2009b) *Making More of Music*, London: Ofsted.

Paechter, C.F. (2000) *Changing School Subjects: Power, Gender, and Curriculum*, Buckingham: Open University Press.

Perkins, D. (1993) Teaching for understanding, *American Educator*, 17(3): 28–35, online available at: www.aea12.k12.ia.us/documents/filelibrary/pdf/iowa_core_curriculum/Teaching_for_Understanding_Article.pdf.

Philpott, C. (2007) Musical learning and musical development, in C. Philpott and G. Spruce (eds), *Learning to Teach Music in the Secondary School*, second edition, London: Routledge.

Pinker, S. (1994) *The Language Instinct*, London: Penguin.

Pirsig, R. (1974) *Zen and the Art of Motorcycle Maintenance*, London: Vintage.

Polanyi, M. (1967) *The Tacit Dimension*, New York: Anchor Books.

Popkewitz, T. (1998) *Struggling for the Soul: The Politics of Schooling and the Construction of the Teacher*, New York: Teachers' College Press.

Porter, A. (2006) Curriculum assessment, in J.I. Green, G. Camilli and P.B. Elmore (eds), *Handbook of Complementary Methods in Education Research*, Mahwah, NJ: Lawrence Erlbaum, pp. 141–60.

Project Zero (2010) *Project Zero*, online, available at: www.pz.harvard.edu [last accessed 17 July 2010].

Proctor, T. (2005) *Creative Problem Solving for Managers: Developing Skills for Decision Making and Innovation*, second edition, London: Routledge.

Pumfrey, P.D. (1993) Cross-curricular elements and the National Curriculum, in G.K.E. Verma and P.D. Pumfrey (eds), *Cross-Curricular Contexts, Themes and Dimensions in Secondary Schools*, London: Falmer Press.

QCA (2009) *Cross-Curriculum Dimensions - A Planning Guide for Schools*, London: QCA.

—— (n.d.) *Guidance for the Diploma Creative and Media: Foundation*, online, available at: www.qcda.gov.uk/resources/assets/Creative_and_media_level_1_new_5B1_5D.pdf

QCA Curriculum Dimensions Website (n.d.): *Creativity and Critical Thinking*, online, available at: http://curriculum.qca.org.uk/key-stages-3-and-4/cross-curriculum-dimensions/creativitycriticalthinking/index.aspx [accessed 19 July 2010].

QCDA (2009) *Disciplined Curriculum Innovation: Making a Difference to Learners*, online, available at: http://orderline.qcda.gov.uk/bookstore.asp?FO=&Action=Book&ProductID=97818 47219299&From=Subject [accessed December 2009].

—— (2010) *A Big Picture of the Secondary Curriculum*, online, available at: http://curriculum.qcda.gov.uk/uploads/BigPicture_sec_05_tcm8-15743.pdf [accessed March 2010].

Raney, K. and Hollands, H. (2000) Art education and talk – from modernist silence to postmodern chatter, in J. Sefton-Green (ed.), *Evaluating Creativity*, London: Routledge.

Reimer, B. (1994) Is musical performance worth saving? *Arts Education Policy Review*, 95(3): 2-12.

Rico, G.L. (1983) *Writing the Natural Way*, Los Angeles, CA: J.P. Tarcher, Inc.

Robinson, K. (2009) Fertile minds need feeding, *The Guardian*, 10 February, online, available at: http://www.guardian.co.uk/education/2009/feb/10/teaching-sats [accessed 21 May 2010].

Ross, A. (2000) *Curriculum: Construction and Critique*, London: Falmer Press.

Russell, B. (1912) *The Problems of Philosophy*, London: Thornton Butterworth.

Russell, J. and Zembylas, M. (2007) Arts integration in the curriculum: a review of research and implications for teaching and learning, in L. Bresler (ed.), *International Handbook of Research in Arts Education Vol. 1*, London: Springer, pp. 287-312.

Ryle, G. (1949) *The Concept of Mind*, Harmondsworth: Penguin Books.

Sachs, J. (2005) Teacher education and the development of professional identity: learning to be a teacher, in P.M.Denicolo and M. Kompf (eds), *Connecting policy and practice: Challenges for teaching and learning in schools and universities*, Abingdon/New York: Routledge, pp. 5–21.

Sadler, D. (1989) Formative assessment and the design of instructional systems, *Instructional Science*, 18(2): 119–44.

Salomon, G. (ed.) (1993) *Distributed Cognitions*, Cambridge: Cambridge University Press.

Savage, J. (1999) *Approaches to Composition with Music Technology in the Key Stage 3 and 4 Curriculum*, online, available at: www.music-journal.com/english/index.htm and follow link to 'Music Lessons' [accessed 20 May 2010].

—— (2002) A digital arts curriculum? Practical ways forward, *Music Education Research*, 4(1): 7–24.

—— (2004) Working towards a theory for music technologies in the classroom: how students engage with and organise sounds with new technologies, *British Journal of Music Education*, 22(2): 167–80.

—— (2005a) *Is Musical Performance Worth Saving?* online, available at: www.music-ite.org.uk/files/articles/musical-performance.pdf [accessed 1 February 2010].

——(2005b) Information communications technologies as a tool for re-imagining music education in the 21st century, *International Journal of Education & the Arts*, 6(2), online, available at: www.ijea.org/v6n2.

—— (2007) Reconstructing Music Education through ICT, *Research in Education*, 78: 65–77.

—— (2010) *New Report on the 'Benefits' of Instrumental Learning*, online, available at: http://jsavage.org.uk/?p=539 [accessed 1 February 2010].

—— (2011) *Cross Curricular Approaches to Teaching and Learning in Secondary Education*, London: Routledge.

—— and Butcher, J. (2007) DubDubDub: improvisation using the sounds of the world-wide-web, *Journal of Music, Technology and Education*, 1(1): 83–96.

—— and Challis, M. (2001)Dunwich revisited: collaborative composition and performance with new technologies, *British Journal of Music Education*, 18(2): 139–49.

Sawyer, R.K. (2003) *Group Creativity: Music, Theater, Collaboration*, Mahwah, NJ: Lawrence Erlbaum.

Schaff, A. (1973) Language and cognition, in R.S. Cohen (ed.) *Linguistics: From Herder to the Theory of the 'Linguistic Field'*, New York: McGraw-Hill.

Scheffler, I. (1999) Epistemology and education, in R. McCormick and C. Paechter (eds), *Learning and Knowledge*, London: Paul Chapman in association with the Open University.

Scruton, R. (1996) Review of Simon Frith – Performing Rites: on the value of popular music, *The Times,* 22 October.

—— (1997) *The Aesthetics of Music*, Oxford: Oxford University Press.

Sebba, J. (2006) Policy and practice in assessment for learning: the experience of selected OECD countries, in J. Gardner (ed.), *Assessment and Learning*, London: Sage.

Sefton-Green, J. (2000) From creativity to cultural production - shared perspectives, in J. Sefton-Green (ed.), *Evaluating Creativity*, London: Routledge.

Sfard, A. (1998) On two metaphors for learning and the dangers of choosing just one, *Educational Researcher*, 27(2): 4–13.

Shulman, L. (1986) Those who understand: knowledge growth in teaching, *Educational Research Review*, 57(1): 4–14.

Spear, M., Gould, K. and Lee, B. (2000) *Who Would be a Teacher? A Review of Factors Motivating and Demotivating Prospective and Practising Teachers*, Slough: NFER.

SSAT website (n.d.) Dylan Wiliam quotation, online, available at: https://secure.ssatrust.org.uk/eshop/default.aspx?mcid=21&scid=31&productid=1325 [accessed April 2010].

Steers, J. (2004) Orthodoxy, creativity and opportunity, *International Journal of Arts Education*, 2(3): 24–38.

Stenhouse, L. (1980) *Curriculum Research and Development in Action*, London: Heinemann Educational.

—— (1983) Research is systematic enquiry made public, *British Educational Research Journal*, 9(1): 11–20.

Stevens, D. (2011) *Cross-Curricular Teaching and Learning in the Secondary School ... English: The Centrality of Language in Learning,* Abingdon: Routledge.

Stobart, G. (2008) *Testing Times - The Uses and Abuses of Assessment*, Abingdon: Routledge.

Strauss, S. (2000) Theories of cognitive development and learning and their implications for curriculum development and teaching, in B. Moon, M. Ben-Peretz and S. Brown (eds), *Routledge International Companion to Education*, London: Routledge.

Suffolk Churches (2010) All Saints, Dunwich, online, available at: www.suffolkchurches.co.uk/dunwichas.html [accessed 15 May 2010].

Sutherland, R. and John, P. (2005) Affordance, opportunity and the pedagogical implications of ICT, *Educational Review*, 57(4): 405–13.

Swanwick, K. (1994) *Musical Knowledge – Intuition, Analysis and Music Education*, London: Routledge.

—— and Taylor, D. (1982) *Discovering Music*, London: Batsford.

Taylor, T. (1999) Movers and shakers: high politics and the origins of the English National Curriculum, in B. Moon and P. Murphy (eds), *Curriculum in Context*, London: Paul Chapman.

TEEVE (2010) *TEEVE Project*, online, available at: http://cairo.cs.uiuc.edu/teleimmersion/ [accessed 13 May 2010].

Théberge, P. (1997). *Any Sound You Can Imagine: Making Music/Consuming Technology*, London: Wesleyan University Press.

Thornton, L. and Brunton, P. (2007) *Bringing the Reggio Approach to Your Early Years Practice*, Abingdon: Routledge.

Troyna, B. and Williams, J. (1986) *Racism, Education and the State*, Beckenham: Croom-Helm.

Tunstall, P. and Gipps, C. (1996) Teacher feedback to young children in formative assessment, *British Educational Research Journal*, 22(4): 389–404.

Van Manen, M. (1977) Linking ways of knowing with ways of being practical, *Curriculum Inquiry*, 6(3): 205–28.

Vygotsky, L. (1978) *Mind in Society*, Cambridge, MA: Harvard University Press.

—— (1987) Thinking and speech, in R.W. Rieber and A.S. Carton (eds), *The Collected works of L.S. Vygotsky*, New York/London: Plenum.

Wallas, G. (1926) *The Art of Thought*, London: Watts.

Waters, S. (1994) *Living Without Boundaries*, Bath: Bath College of Higher Education Press.

Wertsch, J. (2003) Dimensions of culture-clash, in R. Sutherland, G. Claxton and A. Pollard (eds.), *Learning and Teaching: Where World Views Meet*, London: Trentham Books.

Wiggins, J. (2003) Handout from the East Anglian Researchers (EARS) meeting at Homerton College, University of Cambridge.

Wiliam, D. (2000) *Integrating Summative and Formative Functions of Assessment*, keynote address the European Association for Educational Assessment, Prague, November 2000, online, available at: http://eprints.ioe.ac.uk/1151/1/Wiliam2000IntergratingAEA-E_2000_keynoteaddress.pdf.

—— and Black, P. (1996) Meanings and consequences: a basis for distinguishing formative and summative functions of assessment? *British Educational Research Journal*, 22(5): 537–48.

Wilkinson, H. (1996) You can't separate Blur from Schubert, *The Independent*, London.

Young, M. (1999) The curriculum as socially organised knowledge, in R. McCormick and C. Paechter (eds), *Learning and Knowledge*, London: Paul Chapman/Open University.

Zimmerman, B. (2000) Self-efficacy: an essential motive to learn, *Contemporary Educational Psychology*, 25(1): 82–91.

Index